An Alternative Timeline of Indian History

Also by the author:

1. Vedic Physics: Scientific Origin of Hinduism
2. India before Alexander: A New Chronology
3. India after Alexander: The Age of Vikramādityas
4. India after Vikramāditya: The Melting Pot
5. Zero Points of Vedic Astronomy: Discovery of the Original Boundaries of Nakshatras
6. Zero Point of Jain Astronomy: The Origin of Mālava Era

An Alternative Timeline of Indian History

From Buddha and Mahavira to Bappa Rawal

Raja Ram Mohan Roy, Ph.D.

Mount Meru Publishing

Library and Archives Canada Cataloguing in Publication

Title: An alternative timeline of Indian history : from Buddha and Mahavira to Bappa Rawal / Raja Ram Mohan Roy, Ph.D.
Names: Roy, Raja Ram Mohan, 1966- author.
Description: Includes bibliographical references and index.
Identifiers: Canadiana (print) 20200291602 | Canadiana (ebook) 20200291629 | ISBN 9781988207261
(softcover) | ISBN 9781988207254 (HTML)
Subjects: LCSH: East Indians—History.
Classification: LCC DS430 .R69 2020 | DDC 305.800954—dc23

Published in 2020 by:
Mount Meru publishing
P.O. Box 30026, Cityside Postal Outlet PO
Mississauga, Ontario, Canada L4Z 0B6
Email: mountmerupublishing@gmail.com
Web: https://www.mountmerupublishing.com/
Facebook: https://www.facebook.com/MountMeruPublishing
ISBN 978-1-988207-26-1

CONTENTS

PREFACE

The idea for this book came 20 years ago, when I was planning to write a book on astronomical symbolism in Hinduism. During my research, I became aware of the controversy regarding the dating of Varāhamihira. According to Indian tradition, the time of Varāhamihira was first century BCE as he was one of the nine gems in the court of Emperor Vikramāditya, who is associated with the Vikrama era. This era is still in use and has its zero point in 57 BCE. Varāhamihira is currently dated to sixth century CE. When did Varāhamihira live, first century BCE or sixth century CE? The quest to resolve this problem resulted in reevaluating the foundations of Indian history. I have presented my reconstruction of Indian history in my books India before Alexander: A New Chronology, India after Alexander: The Age of Vikramādityas, and India after Vikramāditya: The Melting Pot. I am presenting the information from the above three books into this single concise book for ease of reading. Readers can refer to above three books, if they want to get more detailed information.

Also, during the past three years, I have investigated the dating of Varāhamihira from the position of nakṣatras during summer and winter solstices as specified by him. Currently these positions are assumed to have been true during sixth century CE as that is the time assigned to Varāhamihira. However, if Varāhamihira lived during first century BCE, then the position of nakṣatras specified by him would have been true in first century BCE. This would mean that currently believed nakṣatra boundaries are off by approximately 10°. I have presented the findings of my research in archaeoastronomy carried out for this purpose in two books: "Zero Points of Vedic Astronomy: Discovery of the Original Boundaries of Nakshatras"and "Zero Point of Jain Astronomy: The Origin of Mālava Era."

I would like to express my sincere appreciation to my wife Manju for her continued and enthusiastic support for this work.

Raja Ram Mohan Roy
Mississauga, Ontario, Canada
16 October, 2020

"People are trapped in history and history is trapped in them."
- James Baldwin

1. First Sheet Anchor of Indian History

The timeline of Indian history was constructed during British rule by synchronizing Indian history with Greek history. Colonial era scholars identified two sheet anchors that firmly tie the Indian history to Greek history. Most of the ancient Indian history has been constructed by counting backward and forward from these sheet anchors as shown in Figure 1.1.

The first sheet anchor is the identification of Sandrokottos of the Greek accounts with Chandragupta Maurya, the founder of the Mauryan Dynasty. It was in 1793 CE, when Sir William Jones, President of the Asiatic Society, made this discovery public:

> This discovery led to another of greater moment; for Chandragupta, who, from a military adventurer, became, like Sandracottus, the sovereign of Upper Hindustan, actually fixed the seat of his empire at Pataliputra, where he received ambassadors from foreign princes; and was no other than that very Sandracottus who concluded a treaty with Seleucus Nicator; ... [1]

J.W. McCrindle, compiler of several books detailing the ancient Greek writings on India, described this as a momentous discovery because early Indian history did not have a single chronological landmark of its own [2].

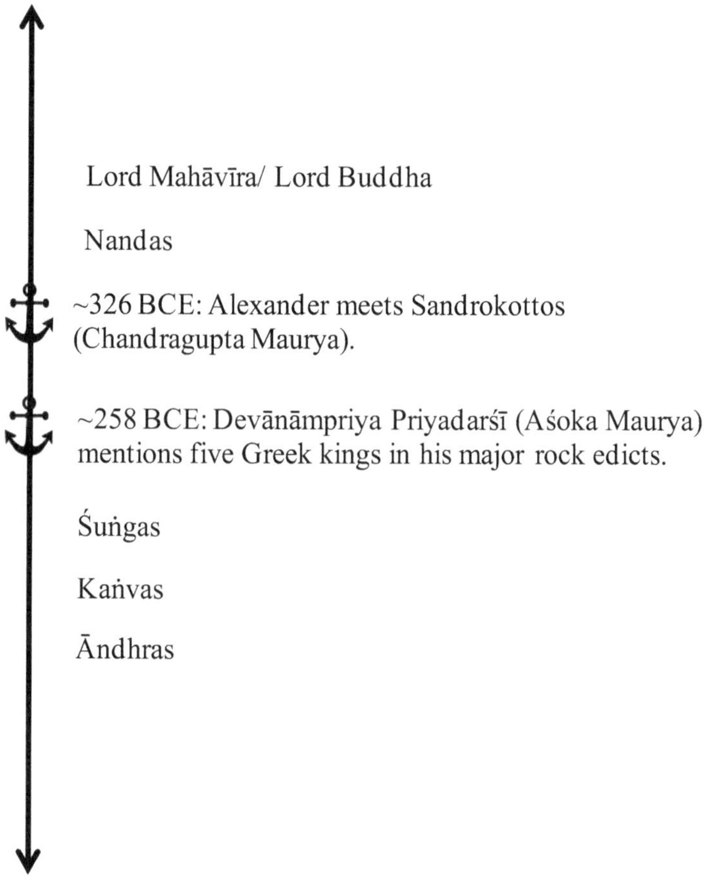
Lord Mahāvīra/ Lord Buddha
Nandas
~326 BCE: Alexander meets Sandrokottos (Chandragupta Maurya).
~258 BCE: Devānāmpriya Priyadarśī (Aśoka Maurya) mentions five Greek kings in his major rock edicts.
Śuṅgas
Kaṅvas
Āndhras

Figure 1.1: The construction of Indian chronology from accepted sheet anchors

However, the identification of Chandragupta Maurya, the founder of the Mauryan Dynasty, with Sandrokottos is not unique. There is another namesake, Chandragupta-I of the Imperial Gupta Dynasty, who could also be the Sandrokottos of the Greek accounts. Currently, Chandragupta Maurya is considered the contemporary of Alexander the Great and Seleucus I Nicator. What if, Chandragupta-I of the Imperial Gupta Dynasty was the contemporary of Alexander the Great and Seleucus I Nicator? Ancient Indian history will then be off by more than six centuries. Chandragupta has been called by various names by Greeks: Sandrokottos by Strabo, Sandrakottos by Pliny, Androkottos by Plutarch [3] and Sandrocottus by Justin [4]. Since the Greek accounts only give the phonetic equivalent of first name Chandragupta and not the last name Maurya, either Chandragupta Maurya or Chandragupta-I of the Imperial Gupta Dynasty could be meant by them. It is then important to examine rest of the evidence to see which Chandragupta fits the Greek accounts better.

1.1 The Predecessor of Sandrokottos

Greek classical writers Diodorus and Curtius respectively have named Xandrames or Agrammes as the ruler of India before Sandrokottos as follows:

> He had obtained from Phegeus a description of the country beyond the Indus: First came a desert which it would take twelve days to traverse; beyond this was the river called the Ganges which had a width of thirty-two stadia, and a greater depth than any other Indian river; beyond this again were situated the dominions of the nation of the Praisioi and the Gandaridai, whose king,

> Xandrames, had an army of 20,000 horse, 200,000 infantry, 2000 chariots, and 4000 elephants trained and equipped for war. [5]
>
> Next came the Ganges, the largest river in all India, the farther bank of which was inhabited by two nations, the Gangaridae and the Prasii, whose king Agrammes kept in the field for guarding the approaches to his country 20,000 cavalry and 200,000 infantry, besides 2000 four-horsed chariots, and, what was the most formidable force of all, a troop of elephants which he said ran up to the number of 3000. [6]

As Curtius, who uses the name Agrammes, belonged to the first century CE, and Diodorus, who uses the name Xandrames, belonged to the first century BCE, it is obvious that Xandrames is the original name, which has been corrupted into Agrammes. Xandrames has been identified by modern historians as the last ruler of the Nanda Dynasty. However, there is no phonetic similarity between the names of Nanda rulers and Xandrames or Agrammes, and it is obvious that this identification is a direct consequence of the identification of Sandrokottos with Chandragupta Maurya. Therefore Greek sources do not support the view that Nandas were ruling India during Alexander's invasion.

1.2 The Successor of Sandrokottos

Greek classical writers have named Amitrochates or Allitrochades as the ruler of India after Sandrokottos as follows:

> Strabo (II.I.9) says: "Both of these men were sent as ambassadors to Palimbothra, - Megasthenes to

> Sandrokottus, Deimachus to Allitrochades, his son; and such are the notes of their residence abroad, which, I know not why, they thought fit to leave. [7]
>
> The Nanda dynasty which was supplanted by the Mauryan in 315 B.C. had succeeded to that of Sisunaga in 370 B.C. Its last member; whom the Greeks call Xandrames and Curtius Agrammes, is variously named in native writings Dhanananda, Nanda MahaPadma, and Hiranyagupta. Xandramas (of which Agrammes seems to be a distorted form) transliterates the Sanskrit Chandramas, which means Moon-god. [8]

First of all, the terms Allitrochades and Amitrochates don't match Bindusāra, son and successor of Chandragupta Maurya, by any stretch of the imagination. Modern history books teach that Bindusāra used the title Amitraghāta ("Slayer of enemies"), the phonetic equivalent of Amitrochates, which is a pure lie. There is no evidence to this effect. If one digs deeper, Patanjali's Mahābhāṣya is cited as the source. However, the word Amitraghāta appears only once in Mahābhāṣya (3.2.87 or 3.2.2.3 depending on classification). Neither Chandragupta nor Bindusara is mentioned in the text of Mahābhāṣya 3.2.87. The word Amitraghāta does not appear in any other ancient Indian text. Thus there is absolutely no evidence from the Indian side that Bindusāra called himself Amitraghāta. Greek side does not refer to the name Bindusāra. So we have a false identification that is being taught as a fact. Amitrochates, the name of the successor of Sandrokottos, is phonetically equivalent to the term "Amitrochchhetā" ("Mower of enemies"), which reminds us of the term "Sarvarājochchhetā" ("Mower of all kings") applied to Samudragupta by his successors [9]. It is plausible that

Samudragupta introduced himself to Greeks as Amitrochchhetā ("Mower of the enemies") reminding the Greeks that enmity with him was going to prove very costly.

1.3 Sandrokottos, the Person Himself

We have seen that the names of the predecessor and the successor of Sandrokottos do not match the predecessor and the successor of Chandragupta Maurya. Let's now analyze the information about Sandrokottos himself as provided by Greek classical writers.

1.3.1 Family Name

We have the following information about the family name of Sandrokottos from the Greek classical writer Strabo:

> The king in addition to his family name must adopt the surname of Palibothros, as Sandrokottus, for instance did, to whom Megasthanes was sent on an embassy. [10]

We do not know the surname of Palibothros, but the most likely intent of the passage was that the name Sandrokottos contained the family name of Sandrokottos. If Sandrokottos was Chandragupta Maurya then this will not hold. However, if Sandrokottos was Chandragupta of the Imperial Gupta Dynasty, then this will fit perfectly as "Gupta", which still is a popular family name in India, was part of the first name of all Imperial Gupta emperors such as Śrīgupta, Ghaṭotkachagupta, Chandragupta-I, Samudragupta, Chandragupta-II, Kumāragupta, Purugupta, Skandagupta and Budhagupta.

1.3.2 Marriage Alliance

Greek classical writer Strabo says the following about Seleucus Nikator and Sandrokottos:

> The Indus runs in a parallel course along the breadth of these regions. The Indians possess partly some of the countries lying along Indus, but these belonged formerly to the Persians. Alexander took them away from the Arianoi and established in them colonies of his own. Seleukos Nikator gave them to Sandrokottus in concluding a marriage alliance, and received in exchange 500 elephants. [11]

Modern historians claim that Seleucus Nikator gave his daughter in marriage to Chandragupta Maurya due to his defeat in the war. This is a direct consequence of the identification of Sandrokottos with Chandragupta Maurya. There is no corroborative evidence for this. In contrast, there is corroborative evidence for the marriage alliance in favour of the identification of Sandrokottos with Chandragupta-I of the Imperial Gupta Dynasty. The son of Chandragupta-I was Samudragupta, who was married to Dattadevī. The first part of the name "Datta" means "given", as in given due to defeat in war. The second part Devī is simply an honourable name for a woman. Thus Dattadevī was the name given after marriage. Samudragupta claims to have earned her using his prowess in the Eran Stone Inscription [12]. This will make perfect sense for a marriage alliance as a result of success in war. We know that Sandrokottos had an encounter with Alexander prior to Alexander's war with King Porus in 326 BCE. The war between Sandrokottos and Seleucus took place in circa 304 BCE. As Chandragupta was a middle-aged man at this time and Samudragupta a young man, the daughter of Seleucus was married to Samudragupta.

1.3.3 Mentor

It is well known that Chandragupta Maurya was installed as the ruler of Magadha by his mentor Chāṇakya, who engineered a coup to depose the last Nanda ruler. Chāṇakya then played a larger than life role as the Prime Minister of Chandragupta, his son Bindusāra, and grandson Aśoka. If Chandragupta Maurya was the Sandrokottos of Greek accounts, then the absence of any mention of Chāṇakya in the Greek accounts is difficult to explain.

1.4 The Coinage

The coinage used by Mauryan rulers was vastly different from the ones used by the Imperial Gupta rulers. Mauryan rulers were using punch-marked coins as quoted below:

> The coins in circulation during the Mauryan period are known as punch-marked coins which neither bear the name of any of the Mauryan rulers nor do they carry any date. Most of these coins have only symbols like tree-in-railing, sun, moon, mountain, animals, birds, etc., punched or stamped on them. [13]

Imperial Gupta rulers are said to have issued gold coins due to earlier rule of Bactrian Greeks as described below:

> It is the Bactrian Greeks who first introduced coins with names and portraits of the rulers who issued them. The figure of the king on the obverse and of a deity or other symbols on the reverse are executed with a high degree of artistic skill. Not only the other foreign hordes who invaded India, but even the Indian rulers adopted the system and issued coins of similar type, though the

> execution is much inferior. The Imperial Guptas issued a series of fine gold coins which, though inferior to those of the Greeks, are yet of high artistic standard. [14]

The question is, if Maurya rulers were contemporaries of Bactrian Greeks, why did they not issue gold coins? They should have been in good contact as Devānāmpriya Priyadarśī, whom historians have identified as Aśoka Maurya, had sent his missionaries to even farther away places like Macedonia and Egypt. However, not only the Mauryan rulers, but long after them the Śuṅga and Kaṇva rulers kept using the punch-marked coins as shown below:

> Magadha issued coinage that may be called India's first national currency which was given the title of imperial type of punch marked coins. Magadha's rule from Pāṭaliputra was followed by that of Nanda, Maurya, Sunga and Kanva dynasties, and all of these dynasties issued punch marked coins of the imperial type. [15]

The conclusion is obvious. Maurya, Śuṅga and Kaṇva dynasties did not issue the gold coins because this technology was unknown to them as their time was several centuries earlier than the time of Bactrian Greeks.

1.5 The Severe Famine

According to Jain sources, there was a great famine during the rule of Chandragupta Maurya:

> Traditional accounts celebrate the place, as the one whereto Bhadrabahu, known as the last Sruttakevalin and preceptor or spiritual guru of Emperor Chandragupta Maurya (321-296 BC) resorted to, leading thousands of lay followers, when the country around Pāṭaliputra had fallen under severe and prolonged famine condition. As

> such, he advised Chandragupta Maurya to make suitable arrangements for mobilization of people, and his Jain sangha, from famine-stricken region, to a safer place. [16]

However, according to the Greek classical writer Diodorus, India had never experienced a famine:

> It is accordingly affirmed that famine has never visited India, and that there has never been a general scarcity in the supply of nourishing food…But, further, there are usages observed by the Indians which contribute to prevent the occurrence of famine among them; for whereas among other nations it is usual, in the contests of war, to ravage the soil, and thus to reduce it to an uncultivated waste, among the Indians, on the contrary, by whom husbandmen are regarded as a class that is sacred and inviolable, the tillers of the soil, even when battle is raging in their neighbourhood, are undisturbed by any sense of danger, for the combatants on either side in waging the conflict make carnage of each other, but allow those engaged in husbandry to remain quite unmolested. Besides, they neither ravage an enemy's land with fire, nor cut down its trees. [17]

If Sandrokottos was Chandragupta Maurya, Greek writers would have known about the severe famine and would not have written that famine had never visited India.

1.6 The List of Kings

Greek classical writers have noted that there were 153 kings between Father Bacchus and Alexander the Great or Dionysos and Sandrokottos, as shown below:

> Their kings from Father Bacchus down to Alexander the Great are reckoned at 153 over a space of 6451 years and three months. [18]

> Father Bacchus was the first who invaded India, and was the first of all who triumphed over the vanquished Indians. From him to Alexander the Great 6451 years are reckoned with 3 months additional, the calculation being made by counting the kings who reigned in the intermediate period, to the number of 153. [19]

> From the time of Dionysos to Sandrakottos the Indians counted 153 kings and a period of 6042 years, ... [20]

Sethna has tabulated the list of kings, but there are only 111 kings starting from Svāyambhūva Manu, the first king in Indian lists, to Chandragupta Maurya, while there are 146 kings, starting from Svāyambhūva Manu to Chandragupta-I [21]. Even though we don't exactly know who the Greeks had in mind when they talked about Father Bacchus or Dionysos, the evidence is clearly against Chandragupta Maurya and in favor of Chandragupta-I of the Imperial Gupta Dynasty being the contemporary of Alexander.

1.7 Traditional Indian History

There is an inconsistency in the Purāṇas as to the exact number of years that passed between the birth of Parīkṣita (shortly after the Mahābhārata war) and the coronation of Mahāpadmananda or Mahānanda, king of the Nanda Dynasty. The variations are 1015, 1050 or 1500 years. However, 1500 years seems to be the right number intended by the authors of the Purāṇas, as they also allocate 1000 years to the dynasty of Bṛhdratha, 138 years to the dynasty of Pradyota, and 362 years to the dynasty of

Śiśunāga since the Mahābhārata war, which adds up to 1500 years [22]. Counting from 3138 BCE as the date of the Mahābhārata war, we get ~1638 BCE for the coronation of Mahāpadmananda. As the Nandas ruled collectively for 100 years, according to the Purāṇas, Chandragupta Maurya started his rule ~1538 BCE. Thus, according to traditional Indian history, Chandragupta Maurya could not have been the contemporary of Alexander the Great.

1.8 Empires: One too many

If Chandragupta Maurya was Alexander's contemporary, then his predecessor – the last Nanda emperor -- was ruling over North India when Alexander attacked Porus. According to the Purāṇas, the Nandas were sole monarchs of their time:

> As son of Mahānandin by a Śūdra women will be born a king, Mahāpadma (Nanda), who will exterminate all kṣatriyas. Thereafter kings will be of Śūdra origin. Mahāpadma will be sole monarch, bringing all under his sole sway. [23]

Since the last of the Nanda rulers was ruling over all of North India at the time of Alexander's invasion, Greek historians should have described a unified North India. On the contrary, they mention two important rulers, one of Prasii and the other of Gangaridai, as mentioned below:

> Next came the Ganges, the largest river in all India, the farther bank of which was inhabited by two nations, the Gangaridae and the Prasii, whose king Agrammes kept in the field for guarding the approaches to his country 20,000 cavalry and 200,000 infantry, besides 2000 four-horsed chariots, and, what was the most formidable force

> of all, a troop of elephants which he said ran up to the number of 3000. [24]

In the light of information presented in this chapter, a new understanding emerges of the state of India during the time of Alexander's invasion and the period after the invasion. The evidence presented shows that Chandragupta-I of the Imperial Gupta Dynasty has better claim for being the contemporary of Alexander the Great instead of Chandragupta Maurya. However, what tilts the balance in favour of Chandragupta Maurya being Sandrokottos is the second sheet anchor of Indian history. We will analyze the evidence for this next.

Notes:

1. Jones (1793): xii-xiv.
2. McCrindle (1877): 7, Footnote.
3. McCrindle (1877): 10.
4. Justinus, Historiarum Philippicarum Libri XLIV, XV.4.19.
5. McCrindle (1893): 281-282.
6. McCrindle (1893): 221-222.
7. Hamilton (1892): 109.
8. McCrindle (1893): 409.
9. Sethna (1989): 246.
10. McCrindle (1901): 42-43.
11. McCrindle (1901): 88-89.
12. Fleet (1888): 20-21.
13. Agnihotry (2010): A-245.
14. Majumdar (1977): 218.

15. Bernholz and Valubel (2014): 54.
16. Subba Reddy (2009): 126.
17. McCrindle (1877): 32-33.
18. McCrindle (1901): 108.
19. McCrindle (1877): 115.
20. McCrindle (1877): 203-204.
21. Sethna (1989): 77-78.
22. Sethna (1989): 5.
23. Pargiter (1913): 69.
24. McCrindle (1893): 221-222.

"History, despite its wrenching pain, cannot be unlived, but if faced with courage, need not be lived again."

- Maya Angelou

2. Second Sheet Anchor of Indian History

The second sheet anchor of Indian history is the identification of Devānāmpriya Priyadarśī of major rock edicts with Aśoka Maurya, the grandson of Chandragupta Maurya. It was Prinsep, who identified Devānāmpriya Priyadarśī with Aśoka Maurya in 1838 [1-2]. The identification of Devānāmpriya Priyadarśī of the inscriptions with Aśoka Maurya of the Mauryan dynasty is the most important sheet anchor of Indian history. It is this identification, which warrants Chandragupta Maurya to be the contemporary of Alexander the Great instead of Chandragupta of Imperial Gupta Dynasty. As Aśoka Maurya is made out to be the contemporary of five Greek rulers during the 3rd century BCE, there remains no doubt that the contemporary of Alexander and Seleucos was Chandragupta Maurya, grandfather of Aśoka Maurya, and not Chandragupta-I of the Imperial Gupta Dynasty, who was posterior to Aśoka Maurya by several centuries.

Any attempt to rewrite Indian history will not succeed unless it can be shown that the identification of

Devānāmpriya Priyadarśī of the inscriptions with Aśoka Maurya is wrong. As this problem is well understood, there have been several attempts in the past to provide alternative explanations. Before we go into the details of these alternatives, we need to first look at the thirteenth rock edict of Devānāmpriya Priyadarśī, which mentions the five Greek rulers supposed to be his contemporaries:

> And this (conquest) has been won repeatedly by Devānāṃpriya both here and among all (his) borderers, even as far as at (the distance of) six hundred yojanas, where the Yona king named Antiyoka (is ruling), and beyond this Antiyoka, (where) four-4-kings (are ruling), (viz. the king) named Turamaya, (the king) named Antikini, (the king) named Maka, (and the king) named Alikasudara, (and) towards the south, (where) the Choḍas and Pāṇḍyas (are ruling), as far as Tāmraparṇī. [3]

We have these five Greek kings mentioned by Devānāmpriya Priyadarśī: Antiyoka, Turamaya, Antikini, Maka and Alikasudara. Their phonetic equivalents are Antiochus, Ptolemy, Antigonus, Magas, and Alexander respectively. If this Devānāmpriya Priyadarśī was not Aśoka Maurya, then who was he?

According to Somayajulu as quoted by Pandit Kota Venkatachelam, Devānāmpriya Priyadarśī was not Aśoka Maurya, but Aśokāditya, another name of Samudragupta:

> The so-called inscriptions of Aśoka do not belong to Aśoka. Most of them do not make any mention of Aśoka. If one or two mention Aśoka they do not refer to Aśoka Vardhana of the Maurya dynasty but they refer to

> Samudragupta of the Gupta dynasty who assumed the title of Aśokāditya. [4]

The problem with this explanation is that there is no evidence whatsoever that Samudragupta ever took the title Aśokāditya and therefore this identification cannot be taken seriously. Additionally, there is no match between the characters of Samudragupta and Devānāmpriya Priyadarśī.

According to another explanation, Antiyoka, Turamaya, Antikini, Maga and Alikasudara are not kings, but the names of regions on the frontiers of ancient India in second millennium BCE [5]. This is the time of Aśoka Maurya according to traditional Indian chronology [5]. Apart from being unconvincing, there is a major problem with this explanation. In April 1958, a rock inscription was found at Shar-i-Kuna near Kandahar in Southern Afghanistan, which is a bilingual inscription in Greek and Aramaic. Prima facie, whoever Devānāmpriya Priyadarśī was, his time was after the invasion of India by Alexander, as this bilingual inscription presupposes the existence of Greek colonies on the frontiers of India. Sethna has presented a feeble explanation that the Greek part of the inscription is a much later addition to the original in Aramaic [6].

Thus so far there has been no solid alternative to the identification of Devānāmpriya Priyadarśī with Aśoka Maurya. If both of them are one and the same then information from the inscriptions of Devānāmpriya Priyadarśī must match the information from literature about Aśoka Maurya.

2.1 Aśoka Maurya vs. Devānāmpriya Priyadarśī

There is plenty of literary information available about Aśoka Maurya. According to Prof. Basham, literary sources for the information on Aśoka are the following: 1. Chronicles of Sri Lanka; 2. Aśokāvadāna as preserved in Divyāvadāna and Chinese versions; 3. Records of Chinese pilgrims; 4. Rājataraṅgiṇī of Kalhaṇa; and 5. Purāṇas [7]. Chronicles of Sri Lanka include Dīpavanśa and Mahāvanśa, while records of Chinese pilgrims include travel notes of Fa-Hien and Yuan Xang. The inscriptions of Devānāmpriya Priyadarśī have been compiled in books such as "Inscriptions of Aśoka" by Hultzsch [8]. We can compare what we know of Aśoka Maurya from literature with what we know of Devānāmpriya Priyadarśī from his inscriptions by consulting these sources and figure out whether both these personalities are one and the same as presented in modern history books.

2.1.1 The Conquest of Kaliṅga

According to Rock edict 13, the conquest of Kaliṅga and the remorse from the ravages of war were the most important events in the life of Devānāmpriya Priyadarśī, but these events find no mention in the literature about Aśoka Maurya. The Kaliṅga war was the turning point in the life of Devānāmpriya Priyadarśī, when he decided to change his ways, preach non-violence, and start following the teachings of Buddhism. There is no mention of Kaliṅga war in the literature about Aśoka Maurya. How can literary sources be silent about the Kaliṅga war, if Aśoka Maurya was Devānāmpriya Priyadarśī? Here is what Prof. Basham, author of "The Wonder that was India", has said:

> One would expect the compilers of this cycle of legends to have recorded the story of the Kalinga war and Aśoka's repentance and embroidered it with many supernatural incidents. Instead, they ignored it. [9]

This is the biggest proof that Aśoka Maurya was not Devānāmpriya Priyadarśī of major rock edicts.

2.1.2 The Conversion to Buddhism

According to Rock edict 13, the Kaliṅga war was the main factor behind the conversion of Devānāmpriya Priyadarśī to Buddhism. However, according to the Mahayana tradition, Aśoka converted to Buddhism due to the patience shown by a Buddhist monk under torture, and according to the Theravada tradition, he was converted by a seven year old monk [10]. Obviously, Devānāmpriya Priyadarśī of major rock edicts was not the same person as Aśoka Maurya.

2.1.3 Third Buddhist Council

According to literary sources, the Third Buddhist Council was held under the patronage of Aśoka Maurya, but there is no mention of it in the edicts of Devānāmpriya Priyadarśī. The absence is very glaring, as Devānāmpriya Priyadarśī describes matters of far less significance in his edicts about what he has done to promote Dharma.

2.1.4 The Family

Aśoka had sent his son Mahendra and daughter Sanghamitrā to Sri Lanka to sprcad Buddhism. There is no mention of them in the edicts of Devānāmpriya Priyadarśī. From the inscription on the Allahabad Pillar, we know that Kāruwākī was the wife of Devānāmpriya Priyadarśī and

Tīvara was their son. However, both Kāruwākī and Tīvara are not mentioned in literary sources about Aśoka Maurya.

In the fifth rock edict, Devānāmpriya Priyadarśī mentions his brothers and sisters, while according to Dipavansa and Mahavansa, Aśoka had killed all his 99 stepbrothers save his own brother Tissa. We have no mention of the killing of step brothers in any of the inscriptions. Also, there is no mention of Tissa in any of his inscriptions. It is strange that there is not a single person that is common to both literary sources about Aśoka Maurya and the inscriptions of Devānāmpriya Priyadarśī.

2.1.5 Vegetarianism

According to Kalhaṇa's Rājataraṅgiṇī (1.101-102), Aśoka was a Jain before he converted to Buddhism. This is also corroborated from Jain accounts. Chandragupta Maurya, grandfather of Aśoka Maurya, was a Jain, who had spent the later days of his life serving the Jain saint Bhadrabāhu. Aśoka's grandson Samprati is considered the "Constantine of Jainism". He did for Jainism what Aśoka did for Buddhism. So if Aśoka's grandfather was a devout Jain, and his grandson was a devout Jain, it is natural to assume that Aśoka Maurya was born a Jain. As Jains and Buddhists are both vegetarians, Aśoka was a vegetarian before and after conversion to Buddhism. However, Devānāmpriya Priyadarśī says in his edicts that before his conversion to Buddhism hundreds of thousands of animals were killed daily in the royal kitchen. This would be incompatible or contradictory information if Aśoka was always a vegetarian, first as a Jain and then as a Buddhist.

2.1.6 Tolerance

Aśoka, who is considered an apostle of non-violence, was not so tolerant even after his conversion to Buddhism. Mukhopadhyaya translates a story from Aśokāvadāna about Aśoka as follows:

> A follower of the Nirgrantha (Mahāvīra) painted a picture, showing Buddha prostrating himself at the feet of Nirgrantha. Aśoka ordered all the Ājīvikas of Pundravardhana (North Bengal) to be killed. In one day, eighteen thousand Ājīvikas lost their lives. A similar kind of incident took place in the town of Pāṭaliputra. A man who painted such a picture was burnt alive with his family. It was announced that whoever would bring the king the head of a Nirgrantha would be rewarded with a Dinara (a gold coin). As a result of this, thousands of Nirgranthas lost their lives. [11]

John S. Strong also narrates this story in his translation of Aśokāvadāna [12]. According to this story, Aśoka was a mass murderer even after his conversion to Buddhism. This is in contrast to the character of Devānāmpriya Priyadarśī, who had completely given up violence after accepting Buddhism.

These facts should create doubts in our minds about Devānāmpriya Priyadarśī and Aśoka Maurya being the same person. If the Devānāmpriya Priyadarśī of the inscriptions does not match the Aśoka Maurya known from literature, then there must be someone else who was the real Devānāmpriya Priyadarśī.

2.2 Face to face with Devānāmpriya Priyadarśī

If Devānāmpriya Priyadarśī was not Aśoka Maurya, and if Aśoka Maurya was a Jain before becoming a Buddhist, we need to search for the real Devānāmpriya Priyadarśī. Based on the fact that the inscriptions of Devānāmpriya Priyadarśī have been found over a wide area covering most of India as well as Bangladesh, Pakistan and Afghanistan, it is obvious that we are not looking for some petty ruler, but someone well-known to historians, though not as Devānāmpriya Priyadarśī. This narrows down the potential number of kings who could be Devānāmpriya Priyadarśī.

I began by scouring books on ancient Indian history in search of Devānāmpriya Priyadarśī. Fortunately, I came across a series of books in Hindi by an accomplished historian, Śrīrāma Goyala, at the Robarts Library, University of Toronto. It was when I was reading his book "Gupta Sāmrājya kā Itihāsa" [13], which translates to "A History of Gupta Empire" that I discovered the correct identity of Devānāmpriya Priyadarśī. In his discussion on the coins of Kumāragupta-I, Śrīrāma Goyala describes fourteen types of coins issued by Kumāragupta-I [14]. The last type of coin is named "Apratigha", which means "not to be vanquished". It has an image in the front of three people. There is a woman on the right side and there is a man on the left side. In the middle, there is an emperor dressed as a monk ("bhikṣu") and it seems that the man and woman are trying to stop him from becoming a monk. It immediately struck me that it was Kumāragupta-I who was the emperor I was searching for. Here is an emperor whose kingdom could have covered the area where the inscriptions of Devānāmpriya Priyadarśī have been discovered from. There is also proof of him becoming a monk, from what we can see in the image imprinted on his coins. It was a tantalizing possibility that needed further investigation.

The next step was to check how long Kumāragupta-I ruled since the rock edicts of Devānāmpriya Priyadarśī mention that some of the edicts were inscribed during the twenty-sixth year of his reign. According to history books, Kumāragupta-I ruled for 40 years: so, there would be no problem in identifying him as Devānāmpriya Priyadarśī. Further conviction was offered after I read the Junagarh rock inscription of Skandagupta in which he describes his father Kumāragupta-I as having attained the friendship of gods. Finally, I was convinced beyond doubt about the identity of Kumāragupta-I as Devānāmpriya Priyadarśī when I read Śrīrāma Goyala's interpretation of a verse from Viṣṇupurāṇa to mean that Kumāragupta-I added Kaliṅga and Māhiṣaka to Gupta territory [15]. Let us now examine the evidence in support of Kumāragupta-I being the Devānāmpriya Priyadarśī of inscriptions.

2.2.1 The Kaliṅga War

The following verse from Viṣṇupurāṇa (4.24.64-65) describes the expansion of the Imperial Gupta Empire:

> Kośala Oḍratāmraliptān Samudrataṭa
> Purīm cha Rakṣito Rakṣyati|
> Kaliṅgam Māhiṣakam Mahendraḥ
> Bhūmau Guham Bhokṣyanti||

Śrīrāma Goyala explains the meaning of this verse as follows [15]:

> (Deva) Rakṣita will expand his domain to Kośala, Oḍra, Tāmralipti and Purī near ocean. Kaliṅga and Māhiṣaka will be under Mahendra. All this land will be ruled by Guha.

Here "rakṣita" stands for Gupta as the meaning of both words is "protected". Kośala was an ancient kingdom located in present day Uttar Pradesh. Oḍra was an ancient kingdom located in the northern part of present day Orissa/Odisha. Tāmralipti was a famous port represented by current day Tamluk in Midnapore district of West Bengal. Purī is the current day Purī district in Odisha. Kaliṅga was an ancient kingdom south of Oḍra located in present day Odisha and northern parts of Andhra Pradesh and Telangana. Māhiṣaka was an ancient kingdom located in present day Karnataka.

Since all the places mentioned in this verse are in eastern and southern part of India except Kośala, it is my contention that Kośala in this verse stands for Dakṣina Kośala, which was an ancient kingdom located in present day Chhatisgarh and Western Odisha. Also, Samudrataṭa, which means ocean shore, may represent the ancient region of Samataṭa located in Southeastern Bengal. Samataṭa is mentioned as one of the regions under the rule of Samudragupta in his Allahabad pillar inscription. Mahendra stands for Kumāragupta-I Mahendrāditya. Guha stands for Skandagupta, as Guha and Skanda are synonyms. Śrīrāma Goyala presumes "Deva" before Rakṣita or Gupta to imply that Devagupta, which is supposedly another name for Chandragupta-II, will expand his domain to Kośala, Oḍra, Tāmralipti and Purī near the ocean. In my opinion, this assumption is not warranted as this important verse gives the following information:

> Gupta (Chandragupta-II) will protect the territories of (South) Kośala, Oḍra, Tāmralipti, Samataṭa and Purī (which are already part of Gupta empire). Kumāragupta-I will expand it further to include Kaliṅga and Māhiṣaka. Skandagupta will enjoy ruling all this land.

Here we have emphatic proof that Kaliṅga was not a part of Gupta Empire ruled by Chandragupta-II, and was conquered by Kumāragupta-I. This is the war that changed Kumāragupta-I, and he accepted Buddhism soon after.

Let us compare this to Aśoka Maurya for whom we have no independent information that he had to fight a war to incorporate Kaliṅga to his empire. In fact, the evidence points to the opposite. Aśoka should have inherited Kaliṅga as it was part of the Nanda Empire, which was taken over by his grandfather Chandragupta-In a coup. He did not have to wage war to capture Kaliṅga. To avoid this situation, modern historians have made up a story about Kaliṅga gaining independence from the Mauryan Empire before the coronation of Aśoka. There is absolutely no evidence to this effect. In fact, there is evidence to the contrary. Chāṇakya is supposed to have served three kings -- Chandragupta, Bindusāra and Aśoka -- according to the medieval text Ārya-Manjuśrī-Mūlakalpa. Noted historian K.P. Jayaswal writes:

> The historical detail about him, which is important, is that he lived in three reigns, triṇi rājyani. Chandragupta seems to have died comparatively young. … Bindusara reigned for 25 years … Chāṇakya must have come down to the opening years of Aśoka, to be the mantrin in three

> reigns. He would have thus maintained the unity of the Maurya policy for over 50 years in his person. [16]

Thus, it would have been very unlikely for Kaliṅga to secede under the watch of Chāṇakya, the man who overthrew the mighty Nanda Empire to avenge Dhana Nanda's insult that he was an ugly-looking man.

2.2.2 The Junagadh Rock Inscription

Skandagupta, son of Kumāragupta-I, says the following in line 4 of the Junagadh rock inscription [17]:

> Pitari sura-sakhitvam prāptvaty ātma- śaktyā

Since this sentence has never been interpreted the way I am going to interpret now, the meaning of each word in this sentence is provided below:

Pitari = father, sura = Gods, sakhitvam = friendship, prāptvaty = obtain, ātma = self and śaktyā = from power

Thus the sentence means that the father obtained the friendship of the Gods by his own power. Historians have taken it to mean that Kumāragupta-I had passed away when this inscription was recorded, as it is customary in India to say that a person has become dear to God when he or she has passed away. However, we need to then ask how could Kumāragupta-I do it with his own power? Did he commit suicide? We don't have any record of that, and if he did commit suicide, why would his son Skandagupta be proudly announcing it? This is nothing to be proud of. What this sentence means is that Kumāragupta-I had obtained the friendship of the Gods by his own power while he was still alive. At least that is what his son Skandagupta was made to believe. Why would he not believe so anyway? His father Kumāragupta-I had declared himself as "Beloved of the Gods" in inscriptions all over the vast empire. He was just paraphrasing the word "Devānāmpriya" meaning "Beloved of the Gods" as "Friend of the Gods". Thus, here we have an acknowledgment from Skandagupta that his father Kumāragupta-I had adopted the name "Beloved of the Gods".

2.2.3 Man of many Names

I will now provide proof that Kumāragupta-I was known as a man with many names as he called himself by other names such as "Devānāmpriya" and "Priyadarśī". Ārya-Mañjuśrī-Mūlakalpa is a text in Sanskrit language written by a Buddhist around 800 CE. It was translated into English by noted historian K. P. Jayaswal. This text gives the following information about the Imperial Guptas:

> Listen about the Medieval and Madhyadesa kings (madhyakāle, madhyamā) who will be in a long period emperors (nṛpendra) and who will be confident and will be followers of via media" (in religious policy, madhyadharmiṇaḥ):
> (1) Samudra, the king,
> (2) Vikrama, of good fame (kīrttitāḥ), 'who is sung'.
> (3)Mahendra, an excellent king and a leader (nṛpavaro Mukhya).
> (4) S-initialled (Skanda) after Ma. (i.e., Mahendra).
> His name (will be) Devarāja; he will have several names (vividhākhya); he will be the best, wise and religious king in that low age. [18]

In this excerpt we find that the first king is Samudragupta; the second king is Chandragupta-II called by the first part of his title Vikramāditya; the third king is Kumāragupta-I identified by the first part of his title Mahendrāditya; and, the fourth king is Skandagupta identified by his initial "S". I would like to draw attention to the description of the king called Devarāja above, who was supposed to have several names. Jayaswal has identified him with Skandagupta [19].

I would like to differ. The author of Ārya-Mañjuśrī-Mūlakalpa is not talking about Skandagupta, but his father Kumāragupta-I. The author says "S-initialled (Skanda) after Ma" and then goes on to say "His name (will be) Devarāja". He continues with the description of M-initialled where the previous sentence ends. It is also clear from the description where he has been called Devarāja, i.e., king of the Gods, which is Indra. Jayaswal says that Skandagupta bore the name of his grandfather (Devarāja), and had a variety of names (virudas). There is absolutely no evidence that Skandagupta bore the name of Devarāja after his grandfather. In the case of Kumāragupta-I it is obvious as his title is Mahendrāditya and he has been called Mahendra by the author of Ārya-Mañjuśrī-Mūlakalpa as quoted above. However, Mahendra (Mahā + Indra) is simply "the great Indra" or Indra himself. Thus it is Kumāragupta-I who has been called Devarāja, and therefore he had a variety of names. This view is also supported by the personal belief of the author of Ārya-Mañjuśrī-Mūlakalpa, who as a Buddhist could not believe that anyone could be a good person without being a Buddhist. This viewpoint becomes obvious by even a cursory reading of the text Ārya-Mañjuśrī-Mūlakalpa.

Jayaswal has made the following comments regarding the description of Chandragupta, Bindusāra, and Chāṇakya in this text.

> Only these two names are given under the dynasty of Chandragupta. Aśoka the Great is already misplaced above. The succession of Bindusāra as a minor is noteworthy, and also his character sketch which was wanting up to this time. He was not a Buddhist. An explanation was therefore due. How could a king be successful without having been a Buddhist? He had as a child raised a toy stūpa of dust. This every Indian child does even to-day. The common form of their play is to raise a mound of dust.
>
> Chandragupta was not a Buddhist. His military career was punished by his illness and poisonous boils.
>
> Chāṇakya has come in for a lot of abuse and deliverance into hell. In his Arthaśāstra he has penalised embracing monkish life without providing for one's family and without state permission. He was hard on Buddhists otherwise. The Buddhist history must have its revenge by assigning such a statesman at least to a long career in hell on paper. [20]

Why would the author of Ārya-Mañjuśrī-Mūlakalpa say good things about Skandagupta, if he is so full of hatred towards non-Buddhists? Skandagupta is not known to have done anything special for Buddhists. The conclusion is obvious. All the encomiums are for Kumāragupta-I as he had not only become a Buddhist, but dedicated his life to spreading Buddhism as proven from his inscriptions as Devānāmpriya Priyadarśī.

2.2.4 Confusion and more Confusion

When Kumāragupta-I started on his mission to be the grand patron of Buddhism, he had the example of Aśoka Maurya to emulate. It seems that historian Kalhaṇa was confused between these two benefactors of Buddhism. According to Kalhaṇa, Aśoka had a son named Jalauka [21]. According to the Tumain inscription, Kumāragupta-I was protecting the earth as if she was his wife. This idea is very unique, and we find that Kalhaṇa used the same description for a king he calls Pratāpāditya whose son is named Jalaukas [22]. It stands to reason that Kalhaṇa was confused between Aśoka Maurya and Kumāragupta-I, and he was not sure whose son Jalauka was. Therefore, he wrote that Aśoka's son was Jalauka and Kumāragupta's son was Jalaukas.

2.2.5 The Prayagraj (Allahabad) Pillar

There are several sets of inscriptions on the Allahabad pillar currently located in the Allahabad Fort including inscriptions by Devānāmpriya Priyadarśī, his queen, and most importantly Samudragupta. There is also an inscription by Moghul Emperor Jahangir on this pillar. Here, my intention is to focus on the inscription by Samudragupta, who according to the modern chronology, was posterior to Devānāmpriya Priyadarśī by over six centuries. Samudragupta was the greatest conqueror known to Indian history. His eulogy inscribed on this pillar gives the details of his conquests and the expanse of his empire. As Samudragupta was posterior to Aśoka Maurya according to modern history, this pillar is known as Aśokan pillar, and Samudragupta's eulogy is supposed to have been inscribed on it later. My contention is to challenge the prevailing wisdom and propose that it was Samudragupta who erected the pillar, and it was Devānāmpriya Priyadarśī's inscriptions that were inscribed later on this pillar. Samudragupta was known for the re-establishment of traditional Vedic/Hindu way of life. There is simply no reason for Samudragupta to have his eulogy inscribed on an existing pillar with inscriptions by a Buddhist king as his zeal for military conquests did not match the pacifist ideology of Devānāmpriya Priyadarśī. Thapar, wondering why Samudragupta chose to write his eulogy on the Aśokan pillar, says that extolling military conquest was contradictory to Aśoka's opposition to violence and if Samudragupta wanted to denigrate Aśoka, it would have been more effective on a separate and equally imposing pillar [23].

It is inconceivable that such a great monarch as Samudragupta, whose generosity was legendary, would use Aśoka Maurya's pillar for writing his eulogy. Samudragupta was so generous as to give away one hundred thousand cows (line 25). He called himself the God of Wealth Kubera (line 26). He further said that his officials were busy returning the wealth of defeated kings everyday (line 26). Why would such a monarch not be able to afford a pillar of his own and choose a pillar erected by Budhist monarch Aśoka Maurya to write his eulogy? Why would he describe an existing pillar as a symbol of his glory? In the lines 29-30 of his inscription on the Allahabad pillar, Samudragupta says with pride that this pillar is looking towards the heaven as the declaration of his glory [24]. On the other hand, Devānāmpriya Priyadarśī, identified as Kumāragupta-I by me, would have been more than happy to add his inscriptions on Samudragupta's pillar as his proud grandson. The realization that Devānāmpriya Priyadarśī wrote his inscriptions on an existing pillar erected by Samudragupta has far reaching implications, and with this single piece of evidence the whole edifice of modern Indian chronology falls like a pack of cards.

2.2.6 Mauryan and Gupta Brāhmī

Inscriptions of Samudragupta and Devānāmpriya Priyadarśī are both written in Brāhmī. According to modern historians, Aśoka Maurya was Devānāmpriya Priyadarśī. So, the inscriptions of Samudragupta are supposed to be written in Gupta Brāhmī and the inscriptions of Devānāmpriya Priyadarśī are supposed to be written in Mauryan Brāhmī. Suppose that Devānāmpriya Priyadarśī was Kumāragupta-I as I have proposed, then both the inscriptions would be written in Gupta Brāhmī. As Kumāragupta-I was the grandson of Samudragupta, there should not really be much of a difference between the scripts used by Samudragupta and Devānāmpriya Priyadarśī. Here is the proof of my proposition:

> Thus, while legends of Aśoka persisted and were transmitted in Buddhist texts and royal lineages were recorded in the Puranas, detailed knowledge of the historical Aśoka and the empire he ruled appears to have been lost relatively rapidly. And by the late fourth century CE, Brahmi script had disappeared from usage. When the Chinese pilgrim Hsuan-tsang visited India in the early seventh century, he recognized the large sculpted columns he saw at several sites as associated with the legendary ruler. But neither he nor earlier

> pilgrims such as Fa-hien were able to read the Aśokan inscriptions on them. [25]

When Fa-hien came to India in the late fourth century CE, as per modern historians Chandragupta-II was ruling. Fa-hien makes no mention of him, which is surprising. What is more surprising is that he could not find anybody who knew Brāhmī. The Imperial Guptas were still using Brāhmī, which may have been somewhat different than Mauryan Brāhmī if we believe modern chronology, but certainly it could not have been so different that nobody could read the inscriptions of Devānāmpriya Priyadarśī. This is consistent with the Imperial Guptas being removed by several centuries in time from Fa-hien so that Brāhmī had no longer been in use for several centuries when Fa-hien visited India.

2.3 Tying the Loose Ends

If Kumāragupta-I was the real Devānāmpriya Priyadarśī of major rock edicts and pillar edicts, then how do we explain the minor rock edicts associating "Devānāmpriya" with Aśoka? The name Aśoka appears in a few minor rocks edicts as "Devānām Piya Aśoka" at Maski in Raichur district, Karnataka, as "Rājā Aśoko Devānāmpiya" at Udegolam in Bellary district, Karnataka and as "Devānāmpiya Piyadasi Aśoka Rājā" at Gujarra near Jhansi, Madhya Pradesh [26]. In addition, versions of minor rock edicts I and II containing the name Aśoka have been found at Nittur in Tumkur district in the state of Karnataka. In order to find a way out of this situation, we will need to understand the meaning of each of these terms and their usages in South Asian literature.

2.3.1 The Meaning of Devānāmpriya

Devānāmpriya means "beloved of the Gods". We find this title being used by many kings. When Prinsep was translating the inscriptions of Priyadarśī, he identified him first with Devānāmpiya Tissa of Ceylon [27-28]. Apart from the inscriptions, this title has been used for other personalities in literature. Devānāmpriya was used as a title by King Daśaratha as well. King Ajātaśatru has been called "Devanuppiya" in "Aupapatika Sūtra". Patañjali, commenting on Pāṇini's Aṣṭādhyāyī 2.4.56, has used this title for a common grammarian. In Indian literature, Kātyāyana in his commentary on Panini's Aṣṭādhyāyī 6.3.21, has said that fools are called Devānāmpriya. It is indeed possible that such uses came into effect due to the Brahmins' dislike of the Buddhists. Also worth noting is the Hindi word "Buddhu" meaning "fool" with its origin in the word "Buddha". Possibly, it was in response to Buddhists making fun of Brahmins by calling them "Brahmabandhu". The point to note is that the title Devānāmpriya was a common title, not a personal name, and could have been used by any king who liked this title.

2.3.2 The Meaning of Priyadarśī

Priyadarśī or Priyadarśana can have two meanings: one who looks handsome, or one who looks with friendliness. Priyadarśī was an adjective that has been used for several kings. In the Rāmāyaṇa, Rāma has been called Priyadarśī once. In the play Mudrārākṣasa, Chandragupta Maurya, grandfather of Aśoka Maurya, has been called Priyadarśī. Gautamīputra Sātakarṇi has been called Priyadarśana in the Nasika inscription. Thus, by itself the use of a title like

Priyadarśī does not make the identification unique, as this title could have been used by other kings as well. There is nothing unique about it.

2.3.3 The Meaning of Aśoka

The word Aśoka is made by joining "A" meaning "no/not" with "Śoka" meaning "sorrow". Thus Aśoka means one who has no sorrow. This raises the possibility that Aśoka may also be used as a title just like Devānāmpriya and Priyadarśī. It need not be a personal name. In Sanskrit literature, the term Priyadarśana has been used as a constant epithet of the Aśoka tree, so much so that Priyadarśana became another name for the Aśoka tree [29].

2.3.4 The five Greek kings

The five Greek kings mentioned in the Rock Edict XIII are: Antiyoka, Turamaya, Antikini, Maka, and Alikasudara. Modern historians have identified them with Antiochus II Theos (261-246 BCE) of Syria and Western Asia, Ptolemy II Philadelphus (285-247 BCE) of Egypt, Antigonus Gonatas (278-239 BCE) of Macedonia, Magas (300-258 or 250 BCE) of Cyrene and Alexander (275-255 BCE) of Epirus or Alexander (252-247 BCE) of Corinth respectively [30].

Based on this information, historians have been able to pinpoint the date of coronation of Aśoka to within a couple of years:

> The latest date at which these kings were reigning together is 258, the earliest 261; and if we could be certain that Aśoka was kept informed of what happened in the West, we might therefore fix the twelfth year of

> his reign between these two years; and hence the date of his coronation between 270 and 273 B.C. [31]

Modern historians have identified all the Greek kings mentioned by Devānāmpriya Priyadarśī and narrowed down to two years, when the Rock Edict 13 was inscribed. It seems that modern historians have the case so foolproof that it is impossible to crack it. However, there has to be something wrong with this picture in the light of what we have discussed in this book so far. Let's take a closer look at the relevant text of Rock Edict 13:

> Antiyoke nāma Yona Rāja paran cha tena
>
> Antiyokena chatura rājāne Turamaye nāma
>
> Antikini nāma Maka nāma Alikasandare nāma [32]

The text has following meaning: "The Greek king named Antiyoka and beyond that king Antiyoka, four kings, named Turamaya, named Antikini, named Maka, named Alikasandara". It is obvious that Devānāmpriya Priyadarśī had close interaction with King Antiyoka or Antiochus and he probably had just heard about the other four Greek kings. When Prinsep first identified King Antiyoka, he had identified him with Antiochus III and not Antiochus II as done by current historians. Why is this of so much importance? Our answer lies in the following quote:

> Furthermore, we have the direct evidence of the historians, above all that of Justin, the epitomator Pompei Trogi, that during the reign of Antiochus II the most important provinces of the east rebelled, an event which must have entirely cut off the connections between Mesopotamia and the borderlands of India until

> these were again, for a very short period of time, restored by Antiochus the Great. [33]

So we find that Antiochus II could not possibly have been the Antiochus mentioned in the major rock edicts. There was no way Antiochus II could have been in touch with Devānāmpriya Priyadarśī. But this is the Antiochus that modern historians have identified as the contemporary of Devānāmpriya Priyadarśī based on the identification of the other four Greek kings mentioned by Devānāmpriya Priyadarśī.

On the other hand, identification of Antiyoka with Antiochus III fits perfectly with the identification of Kumāragupta-I with Devānāmpriya Priyadarśī. Starting with Chandragupta-I as a contemporary of Alexander the Great, the reign of Kumāragupta-I will overlap with the reign of Antiochus III about whom we have definite information that he arrived at the border of India. If Antiochus III the Great was the contemporary of Devānāmpriya Priyadarśī, how do we account for the other four kings, all of whom were certainly not ruling during the revised time period of Kumāragupta's rule (213-173 BCE)? The answer has been provided by Professor H.H. Wilson, Director of the Royal Asiatic Society, in 1850 CE itself as follows:

> We must look, therefore, not to dates, but to the notoriety of the names, and the probability of their having become known in India, for the identification of the persons intended. Under this view, I should refer Alexander to Alexander the Great, Antigonus to his successor, Magas to the son-in-law of Ptolemy Philadelphus, Ptolemy to either or all of the four first

> princes of Egypt, and Antiochus to the only one of the number, who we know from classical record did visit India, who from the purport of the inscriptions we may infer was known there personally, Antiochus the Great. In this case we obtain for the date of the inscription some period subsequent to B.C. 205, at which it seems very unlikely that Aśoka was living. [34]

The views of Prof. Wilson, which have been neglected by current historians in favor of the accepted chronology, need to be taken seriously. We need to understand that all the Greek kings mentioned by Devānāmpriya Priyadarśī were not his contemporaries. If someone asks me here in Canada -- "Where are you from?" and I say, "I am from the land of Swāmī Vivekānanda", does it make me the contemporary of Swāmī Vivekānanda? If we look at this carefully, how could Devānāmpriya Priyadarśī be so current about far away kings of distant lands? How can the period of the writing of Rock Edict 13 be specified within a narrow range of time of two years? Kings could change by the time information reached Devānāmpriya Priyadarśī. In fact, Devānāmpriya Priyadarśī accepts in Rock Edict II that he did not know the names of the four kings who reigned beyond the land of Antiochus by saying "Yona king named Antiyoka, and the other kings who are the neighbours of this Antiyoka." Thus the correct purport of Rock Edict XIII is "where the Yona king named Antiyoka (is ruling) and beyond this Antiyoka, **(the land of)** four kings (the king) named Turamaya, (the king) named Antikini, (the king) named Maka, (and the king) named Alikasudara". Thus while Antiochus was definitely his contemporary, the other four kings -- Ptolemy, Antigonus, Magas and Alexander -- were either his contemporaries or before his time.

It follows from my reasoning that the extent of the Imperial Gupta Empire was much larger than the extent of the Maurya Empire, which is drawn by enclosing the areas where the inscriptions of Devānāmpriya Priyadarśī have been found. In fact, what is shown as the extent of the Maurya Empire in textbooks is the extent of the Imperial Gupta Empire. As Devānāmpriya Priyadarśī was Kumāragupta-I and not Aśoka Maurya, the actual extent of the Maurya Empire will be hard to demarcate.

The identification of Sandrokottos with Chandragupta-I and Devānāmpriya Priyadarśī with Kumāragupta-I, both of the Imperial Gupta Dynasty, frees Indian history from the shackles of the current chronology and provide us the opportunity to reconstruct the history of India as it really happened. We will start with the dating of Lord Buddha.

Notes

1. Prinsep (1838a).
2. Prinsep (1838b).
3. Hultzsch (1925): 27-71.
4. Venkatachelam (1953): 8.
5. Vyāsaśiṣya (1988): 181.
6. Sethna (1989): 359.
7. Basham (1982).
8. Hultzsch (1925): 27-71.
9. Basham (1982).
10. Basham (1982).
11. Mukhopadhyaya (1963): xxxvii.

12. Strong (1989): 232.
13. Goyala (1987a).
14. Goyala (1987a): 244-246.
15. Goyala (1987a): 253.
16. Jayaswal (1934): 17.
17. Fleet (1888): 56-65
18. Jayaswal (1934): 33.
19. Jayaswal (1934): 35-36.
20. Jayaswal (1934): 16-17.
21. Rājataraṅgiṇī 1.101-108.
22. Rājataraṅgiṇī 2.5-9.
23. Thapar (2013): 341.
24. Goyala (1987b): 16-19.
25. Alcock (2001): 161.
26. Vassilkov (1997-98).
27. Prinsep (1837).
28. Hultzsch (1914): 943-951.
29. Vassilkov (1997-98).
30. Sethna (1989): 233.
31. Davids (1877): 42.
32. Hultzsch (1925): 86-87.
33. Charpentier (1931).
34. Wilson (1850). Excerpts from pages 244-247.

"What you are is what you have been. What you'll be is what you do now."
- Buddha

3. The Dating of Buddha

Due to the central position of Lord Buddha in ancient Indian history, it is of paramount importance to correctly fix his date. Lord Buddha is the most dynamic and mesmerizing personality from ancient India. A number of dates for Lord Buddha have been proposed depending on the source of information. A good summary of these proposed dates was presented in a conference paper by Siglinde Dietz titled "The Dating of the Historical Buddha in the History of Western Scholarship up to 1980" [1]. The earliest dating of the Lord Buddha known to Europeans was presented in the work Confucius Sinarum Philosophus sive scietia Sinesis Latine exposita in 1687. This book was compiled by 17 Jesuits and gave the year 1026 BCE as the birth of the Lord Buddha and dated his Nirvāṇa to 947/46 BCE. In 1738 Capuchin monk Father Francesco Orazio della Penna gave 959 BCE as the year of Lord Buddha's birth. In 1756 Joseph Deguignes wrote in "Histoire generale des Huns, des Turcs, des Mongols, et des autres Tartares occidentaux" that according to the majority of historians, Lord Buddha was born in Kashmir around the year 1027 BCE. In 1788 Sir William Jones weighed the various sources and accepted 1027 BCE as the date of the

Lord Buddha's birth. In 1799 Francis Buchanan presented a number of dates for Lord Buddha's life, 1028 BCE according to Chinese, 544 BCE according to Siamese and 542 BCE according to Singhalese. In 1805 J.H. Harrington considered the Singhalese date to be credible as the Singhalese sacred era was reckoned from it and the date matched Siamese era very well. In 1823 Julius Heinrich Klaproth presented the following list of dates of Lord Buddha's birth according to various traditions: 961 BCE according to Mongolian, 1027 BCE according to Chinese, between 1029 to 960 BCE according to Japanese, 1366 BCE according to Abul Fazl and 2009 BCE according to a Hindu work Bhāgavatāmṛta. In 1825 Wilson calculated 1332 BCE as the date of Nirvāṇa of Lord Buddha according to Kalhaṇa's Rājataraṅgiṇī.

Thus we see that there were a number of dates for the year of birth of Lord Buddha with majority of them being around or before 1000 BCE. Purāṇas give the earliest dates for the birth of Lord Buddha. As quoted above, one work Bhāgavatāmṛta gave 2009 BCE as the year of birth of Lord Buddha based on Purāṇas. This was the work that was quoted by Pandit Rādhākānta to Sir William Jones in eighteenth century:

> On my demanding written evidence, he produced a book of some authority, composed by a learned Goswami, and entitled Bhagawatamarita, or the Nectar of the Bhagawat, on which it is a metrical comment; and the couplet which he read from it deserves to be cited. [2]

The dates of Lord Buddha based on Purāṇas do not match though. While Bhāgavatāmṛta gave the year of birth of Lord Buddha as 2009 BCE, Pandit Kota Venkatachelam calculated the year of birth to be 1887 BCE [3]. However, it can be safely said that the year of birth of Lord Buddha is closer to 2000 BCE according to the Purāṇas.

The currently accepted year of birth of Lord Buddha was calculated based on the identification of the Indian king Sandrokottos from Greek accounts with Chandragupta Maurya by Sir William Jones in 1793 CE [4]. Most of the modern historians place the birth of Lord Buddha in the sixth century BCE (sometime between 567-563 BCE) and his Nirvāṇa in the fifth century BCE (sometime between 487-483 BCE). Since Indian and Chinese dates are too early, modern historians have argued that Singhalese/Sri Lankan dates are the most reliable. However, what the historians have fed us as most reliable also results in a chronological dilemma that is impossible to resolve. This problem has been stated by Theodor Benfey in 1839 in the following words:

> … all Ceylonese chronicles begin their history with the year 543 B.C., the Nirvāṇa of Gautama Buddha. … we can hardly place the beginning of Chandragupta's reign earlier than 312 B.C. According to the chronology of Mahavamsa, however, Chandragupta's accession to power dates to the year 381 B.C. The difference thus amounts to 69 or 70 years. One can see from this that two types of dates – one pertaining to Indian history and others to the life of the Buddha – are joined in a synchronism, without matching up. [1]

Let me explain this problem further. Modern historians have calculated the date of the Lord Buddha from the date of Aśoka Maurya, whose date of coronation has been fixed at ~268 BCE, based on his identification with

Devānāmpriya Priyadarśī. According to Singhalese texts the coronation of Piyadassi took place 218 years after the Nirvāṇa of the Lord Buddha and therefore the Nirvāṇa of Lord Buddha took place at ~486 BCE. This will place the year of his birth 80 years earlier at ~566 BCE. However, the same Singhalese texts that mention 218 years between the Nirvāṇa of Lord Buddha and coronation of Piyadassi are also emphatic that Nirvāṇa of Lord Buddha took place in 543 BCE. Counting from this date the coronation of Aśoka Maurya took place 218 years later in 325 BCE, which is around the time of the invasion of India by Alexander. This will make Aśoka Maurya the contemporary of Alexander instead of his grandfather Chandragupta Maurya, who must be placed 50 years earlier in 375 BCE. Chandragupta Maurya can then no longer be the contemporary of Alexander and the identification of Sandrokottos of Greek accounts with Chandragupta Maurya fails.

Modern historians are telling us that the place farthest from the birthplace of Lord Buddha has preserved the most authentic date of his birth. There is simply no reason for Singhalese texts to be more reliable than Indian, Chinese, and Nepalese texts. It is more likely that the most authentic information about the birth of Lord Buddha was preserved in a place closer to his place of birth. I would like to propose that this has indeed been the case and this information is to be found in an astronomical text called the Sumatitantra, the first book on astronomy from Nepal. The relevant verses from Sumatitantra are presented and discussed in a paper titled "Mānadeva Samvat: An investigation into an Historical Fraud" by Kamal P. Malla

[5]. We should note the title of the paper, which is symptomatic of the attitude that modern historians have towards our ancient records. The objective is not to understand what they mean but to declare as forgery whatever does not suit the accepted chronology. What is being dismissed as a historical fraud not only provides information about the date of Lord Buddha, but also provides evidence in support of the Imperial Guptas being contemporary of Alexander. In addition, it provides the identification of Emperor Śudraka, whose writing Mṛchchhakaṭikam is well known (Film Utsava was based on it), but whose identity is unknown. Sumatitantra contains the following verses:

> jāto duryodhano rājā kalisandhyam pravarttate |
> Yudhiṣṭhiro mahārājo duryodhanastayopi vā ||
> ubhau rājau sahasre dve varṣantu sampravarttati |
> Nandarājyam śatāṣṭañchaśchandraguptastatopare ||
> rājyaṅkaroti tenāpi dvātriṃśachchādhikaṃ śatam |
> rājā Śūdrakadevaścha varṣasaptābdhi chāśvinou ||
> Śakarājā tatopaśchādvasurandhra kritantathā |
> ityate bhāṣitammahyam jnayā rājā krameṇa tu ||
> Śesā yutāścha kṛta ambarāgni 304 Śrī Mānadevābda prayujyamānā
> etāni piṇḍa kalı varṣamahuḥ ||

We can extract the following information from these verses:

> Yudhiṣṭhira and Duryodhana were present at the junction of Kali (with Dwāpara). Both of them continued for 2000 years, Nanda ruled for 800 years, Chandragupta for 132 years, Śūdraka for 247

> years, Śaka king for 498 years and Mānadeva for 304 years.

The intended meaning of these verses will be obvious to those familiar with Indian tradition, but these verses will be incomprehensible to those not familiar with the tradition. Malla says the following about these verses:

> The above text has been transcribed, translated, and interpreted differently by different Nepali and foreign historians of Nepal, depending upon how, for instance, one translates the word, sampravarttate. Yet the fact remains that not a single of the figures for the six epoch eras mentioned in the Sumatitantra – (Yudhiṣṭhira 2000, Nanda 800, Chandragupta 132, Śūdraka 247, Śaka 498, and Mānadeva 304) matches with the known historical facts. … If the intention was to specify the duration of a king's reign or rule, then it is clearly a pious fabrication. [5]

Let's try to understand what these verses mean. It is quite obvious that these verses are not defining the ruling period of kings as no one lives for 2000 years. These verses are not defining how long the individual eras lasted, as the use of Śaka era is still continuing. What is being defined is the period between the eras listed in these verses and this yields the following very important information: The Nanda era started 2000 years after the Kali era. The Chandragupta era started 800 years after the Nanda era. The Śūdraka era started 132 years after the Chandragupta era. The Śaka era started 247 years after the Śūdraka era. The Mānadeva era started 498 years after the Śaka era. The text Sumatitantra was written in the 304th year of the Mānadeva era.

It is well established that the Kali era started in 3102 BCE. Therefore, according to these verses, the Nanda era started in 1102 BCE, the Chandragupta era started in 302 BCE, the Śudraka era started in 170 BCE, the Śaka era started in 78 CE, the Mānadeva era started in 576 CE, and the text Sumatitantra was written in 880 CE in the 304th year of the Mānadeva era. Since there was no zero BCE or zero CE and 1 CE followed 1 BCE, 247 years from 170 BCE falls in 78 CE instead of 77 CE. We should note that the starting date of the well-known Śālivāhana Śaka era is 78 CE, and this calculation exactly matches with it. This provides a solid confirmation for this interpretation. Since Nanda is separated by 800 years from Chandragupta, this Chandragupta has to belong to Imperial Guptas as Chandrgupta Maurya was close successor to Nanda. This verse then places Chandragupta of Imperial Gupta dynasty in 302 BCE making Imperial Guptas contemporary of Alexander and his successors instead of Mauryas.

The date of the Lord Buddha can be calculated from the information on the Nanda era provided by Sumatitantra as follows. We will use the following information from the Purāṇas for this purpose as given by Pargiter [6].

> Ajātaśatru will be king 25 years. Darśaka will be king 25 years. After him Udāyin will be king 33 years. That king will make as his capital on the earth Kusumpura on the south bank of the Ganges in his fourth year. Nandivardhana will be king 40 years. Mahānandin will be 43 years. ... As son of Mahanandin by a śudra woman will be born a king, Mahapadma (Nanda), who will exterminate all kśatriyas. Thereafter kings will be of Śudra origin. Mahapadma will be sole monarch,

> bringing all under his sole away. He will be 88 years on the earth. He will uproot all kśatriyas, being urged on by prospective fortune. He will have 8 sons, of whom Sukalpa will be the first; and they will be kings in succession to Mahapadma for 12 years. A Brahman Kautilya will uproot them all; and, after they have enjoyed the earth 100 years, it will pass to the Mauryas. [6]

There are three Nandas in this list, Nandivardhana, Mahānandin, and Mahāpadma Nanda. We need to decide which one is intended in this text. To make the proper choice, we need to keep in mind that Lord Mahāvīra and Lord Buddha were contemporaries. In the next chapter, I provide information for dating Lord Mahāvīra's birth in 1244 BCE. To be consistent with this date, the Nanda era needs to start with the beginning of the reign of Nandivardhana. Based on this assumption, the chronology of Magadha kings is shown in Table 3.1.

Table 3.1: The chronology of Magadha kings

King	Reign in years	Proposed Chronology
Ajātaśatru	25	1185-1160 BCE
Darśaka	25	1160-1135 BCE
Udāyin	33	1135-1102 BCE
Nandivardhana	40	1102-1062 BCE
Mahānandin	43	1062-1019 BCE
Mahāpadma Nanda and Eight Nandas	100	1019-919 BCE

Lord Buddha died during eighth year of Ajātaśatru's reign [7]. Thus, the Parinirvāṇa of Lord Buddha took place in 1178 BCE, based on information presented in Table 3.1. As Lord Buddha had lived for 80 years, he lived between 1258-1178 BCE.

It is not a coincidence that the most authentic information about the year of birth of Lord Buddha and the era of Imperial Guptas is preserved in a text from Nepal. While Lord Buddha was born in present day Nepal, Chandragupta-I married a Lichchhavi princess and Lichchhavis had moved to Nepal subsequent to the rise of the Imperial Guptas. It means that the history of Nepal is also as messed up as that of India with Lichchhavis moving to Nepal around six centuries earlier than currently believed. A way out of the resulting confusion has been found by declaring genuine documents as forgery instead of re-examining the faulty chronology.

As we have seen in this chapter, the information that has come to us from our ancestors may be in a cryptic form. If we don't have the patience and attitude to understand the information, it will seem incomprehensible. We are inheritors of a unique civilization that has survived the ravages of time because it devised ways to preserve its knowledge base not only through literature but also through popular traditions. If we carefully analyze the information, we will find that the true history of India is completely different from what is accepted right now. We will examine thc dating of Lord Mahāvīra next.

Notes:

1. Dietz (1995): 39-105.
2. Jones (1788).
3. Venkatachelam (1956): 17.
4. Jones (1793).
5. Malla (2005).
6. Pargiter (1913): 69.
7. Majumdar, Pusalker, and Majumdar (2001): 37.

"All human beings are miserable because of their own ignorance, and they themselves can be happy by acquiring proper knowledge."

- Mahāvīra

4. The Dating of Mahāvira

According to well established Jain traditions given in Paṭṭāvalīs, the Nirvāṇa of Lord Mahāvīra took place 470 years before Vikram era. Jain texts provide breakdown of the intervening period as shown in Table 4.1 [1]:

Counting from 57 BCE, this gives 527 BCE as the year of Nirvāṇa of Lord Mahāvīra. Since Lord Mahāvīra lived for 72 years, he lived between 599 BCE to 527 BCE according to Jain traditions. This creates a problem for modern historians as they have placed the birth of Lord Buddha sometime between 567-563 BCE and his Nirvāṇa sometime between 487-483 BCE. The Nirvāṇa of Lord Mahāvīra more than 40 years before Lord Buddha would make him too much senior than Lord Buddha, so they had to bring the date of Lord Mahāvīra closer to the date of Lord Buddha. Jacobi had achieved that by proposing that the period between the Nirvāṇa of Lord Mahāvīra and Vikram era should not include the 60 years of Pālaka:

> Pālaka had, most probably, no place in the original chronology of the Jains. He is, I am inclined to believe, a mere chronological fiction of the Jains introduced in

order to make it better agree with the Buddhist chronology of Ceylon. [2]

Table 4.1: Kings after the Nirvāṇa of Lord Mahāvīra

King	Reign period
Pālaka	60 years
The Nandas	155 years
The Mauryas	108 years
Puṣyamitra	30 years
Balamitra-Bhānumitra	60 years
Naravāhana	40 years
Gardabhilla	13 years
Śaka	4 years
Total	470 years

The argument is really strange, because it is the modern historians who have put so much faith in the Buddhist chronology of Ceylon and derived the date of Lord Buddha from Ceylonese chronicles. Why would Jains of India have bothered about the belief of the Buddhists in Ceylon? Based on this spurious argument of neglecting the rule of Pālaka, the coronation of Chandragupta Maurya is taken 155 years after the Nirvāṇa of Lord Mahāvīra. The coronation of Chandragupta Maurya took place 255 years before Vikrama era according to the list above, or in 312 BCE. The Nirvāṇa of Lord Mahāvīra is thus placed in 467 BCE and his birth 72 years earlier in 539 BCE. The whole argument totally neglects the other piece of information in Jain texts according to which Lord Mahāvīra's Nirvāṇa coincided with the coronation of Pālaka, who had ruled for sixty years. Another variation of this force-fitting of evidence has been given by Seth, who has argued that Lord Mahāvīra's Nirvāṇa took place in 488 BCE [3]. To arrive at this date, he simply neglects the rule of Naravāhana, thus deducting 40 years from the 470 year interval between the Nirvāṇa of Lord Mahāvīra and Vikram era. Counting from 58 BCE as the beginning of Vikram era instead of 57 BCE and assuming 430 years between the Nirvāṇa of Lord Mahāvīra and Vikram era instead of 470 years, he arrives at 488 BCE as the year of the Nirvāṇa of Lord Mahāvīra. The aim is to show that the Nirvāṇa of Lord Mahāvīra took place before the Nirvāṇa of Lord Buddha as implied by some Buddhist texts. The evidence to this effect is not very solid though as pointed out by Basham:

> We suggest that the Pāli record may not in fact refer to the death of Mahāvīra at Pāvā, but to that of Gosāla at Sāvatthi, which the Bhagavatī Sūtra also mentions as having been accompanied by quarrelling and confusion. At a later date, when the chief rival of Buddhism was no longer Ājīvikism but Jainism, the name may have been altered to add to the significance of the account. [4]

Having shown that the current dating of Lord Mahāvīra by modern historians is arbitrary, let's try to derive a new date of Lord Mahāvīra based on Jain traditions. Our most important clue is that Jain traditions held that the Nirvāṇa of Lord Mahāvīra took place 470 years before Vikram era. It is my proposition that over the course of more than two millennia Jains have substituted Mālava era with Vikram era as they are both related to the history and legends of Vikramāditya. According to modern historians, both Mālava era and Vikram era are identical. In fact, the history books teach us that there is another era, Kṛta era that is identical to both Mālava era and Vikram era. The question is how do they know that? There is an inscription of Aulikara king Naravarman written in year 461 in which Mālava era has been called Kṛta era [5], but there is no inscription that equates either Mālava era or Kṛta era with Vikram era.

The zero point of Mālava Era has to have some relation to the region known as Malwa. The most obvious connection is to the story of Vikramāditya, who was the emperor of Malwa region according to Hindu-Jain traditions. Vikramāditya ruled from the city of Ujjayinī, the capital of Malwa region. The legend of Vikramāditya is based on the reversal in the path of sun at Ujjayinī. Traditionally, it is assumed that the word Vikramāditya is composed by joining the words "Vikrama" and "Āditya". Vikrama means valour, and Āditya means Sun, and thus the meaning of Vikramāditya is the "Sun of Valour" or "Brave as the Sun". However, this was not the intended meaning behind the legend of Vikramāditya. The word Vikramāditya can also be composed by joining the prefix "Vi" with the words "Krama" and "Āditya". The prefix "Vi" imparts the meaning of deviation or opposite to the word that follows it. For example, the word "Vikāra" means creating deviation and hence connotes degradation. The word "Kraya" means to buy and the word "Vikraya" means to sell. The word "Krama" means "order" and "Āditya" of course means the Sun. Putting it all together, Vikramāditya means deviation in the order of the Sun. Let us ponder at what happens to the Sun at Ujjayinī. As days grow longer, the Sun moves northwards towards Ujjayinī and continues till the day of the summer solstice, on which day the Sun stands vertically up at Ujjayinī. The next day the Sun reverses its journey and starts going south. This fact that the Sun changes its course at Ujjayinī, formed the basis of the legend of Vikramāditya. Due to its location at the Tropic of Cancer Ujjayinī became the most prominent centre for astronomical research in ancient India and the prime meridian of the ancient world in the manner of Greenwich today. This intimate connection between Vikramāditya and Malwa region became the reason for the confusion between Mālava era and Vikrama era.

As both the Mālava era and the Vikrama era have Jain origins, Jain authors later got confused between these eras. They had the memory of the era starting 470 years after the Nirvāṇa of Lord Mahāvīra. I have proposed in my book "Zero Point of Jain Astronomy: The Origin of Malava Era" that the zero point of Mālava Era was in 702 BCE [6]. If we count 470 years from the beginning of Mālava era in 702 BCE, the Nirvāṇa of Lord Mahāvīra took place in 1172 BCE. As Lord Mahāvīra had lived for 72 years, he lived between 1244-1172 BCE. This new date is consistent with the evidence that Lord Buddha and Lord Mahāvīra were contemporaries. We will take up the chronology of India after Lord Buddha and Lord Mahāvīra next.

Notes:

1. Pandeya (1951): 26.
2. Eggermont (1968): 69.
3. Jain (1991): 77-78.
4. Basham (1951): 75.
5. Shastri (1996): 35-65.
6. Roy (2020)

"When our false perception is corrected, misery ends also."

- Ādi Śankarāchārya

5. India after Buddha and Mahāvīra

As we have discussed, colonial era historians considered Chandragupta Maurya to be the contemporary of Alexander the Great and Aśoka Maurya to be the contemporary of the Greek kings mentioned in the rock edicts of Devānāmpriya Priyadarśī. I have shown that these sheet anchors need to be changed. Chandragupta-I of the Imperial Gupta Dynasty was the contemporary of Alexander the Great and Kumāragupta-I was the contemporary of some of the Greek kings mentioned in the rock edicts of Devānāmpriya Priyadarśī. This means that chronology of ancient India has been pushed forward by over six centuries. In the previous two Chapters, the dating of Lord Buddha and Lord Mahāvīra has been calculated from independent considerations that are consistent with the alternative sheet anchors. Table 5.1 presents the alternative chronology of the kings of Magadha from the time of the Buddha and Mahāvīra to the end of the Nanda Dynasty as compared to the accepted chronology. The justification for these dates has been provided in Chapter 3.

Table 5.1: The chronology of pre-Maurya kings

Kings	Reign in years	Accepted Chronology [1]	Proposed Chronology
Bimbisāra	52	544-492 BCE	1237-1185 BCE
Ajātaśatru	25	492-460 BCE	1185-1160 BCE
Darśaka	25		1160-1135 BCE
Udāyin	33	460-444 BCE	1135-1102 BCE
Udāyin's successors		444-412 BCE	
Nandivardhana	40		1102-1062 BCE
Śiśunāga dynasty		412-344 BCE	
Mahānandin	43		1062-1019 BCE
Mahāpadma Nanda	88	344-323 BCE	1019-919 BCE
Eight Nandas	12		

The chronological framework developed in this book gives us the opportunity to correctly date the scholars from the remote past. Vararuchi is a famous name in Sanskrit literature. Vararuchi was the author of many literary and scientific texts. Pāṇini is well known for the treatise on Sanskrit grammar called Aṣṭādhyāyī.

Ārya-Mañjuśrī-Mūlakalpa offers the following information about Vararuchi and Pāṇini:

> After him there will be king Nanda at Pushpa-city. … His minister was a Buddhist Brahmin Vararuchi who was of high soul, kind and good. The king, though true, caused alienation of feeling of the Council of Ministers at Patala City (434-35). The king became very ill, died at 67. His great friend was a Brahmin, Panini by name. [2]

They both adorned the court of King Nanda, who could be Nandivardhana, Mahānandin, Mahāpadma Nanda or any of the eight Nanda kings. Thus we can tentatively fix the time of these two luminaries to 11th-10th century BCE.

5.1 Magadha after Nandas

It is well known that the last Nanda king was deposed by Chandragupta Maurya, who established the Maurya dynasty. He became the emperor with the help of Chāṇakya, a Brāhmaṇa who was humiliated by the last Nanda king. The chronology of the kings of Magadha after Nandas can be determined from the regnal years given in the Purāṇas:

> Kauṭilya will anoint Chandragupta as king in the realm. Chandragupta will be king 24 years. Vindusāra will be king 25 years. Aśoka will be king 36 years. His son Kuṇāla will reign 8 years.
>
> Kunāla's son Bandhupālita will enjoy the kingdom 8 years. Their grandson Daśona will reign 7 years. His son Daśaratha will be king 8 years. His son Samprati will reign 9 years. Śāliśūka will be king 13 years. Devadharman will be king 7 years. His son Śatadhanvan will be king 8 years. Bṛhadratha will reign 70 years. These are the 10 Mauryas who will enjoy the earth full 137 years. After them it will go to the Śuṅgas.
>
> Puṣyamitra the commander-in-chief will uproot Bṛhadratha and will rule the kingdom as king 36 years. His son Agnimitra will be king 8 years. Vasujyeṣṭha will be king 7 years. His son Vasumitra will be king 10 years. Then his son Andhraka will reign 2 years. Pulindaka will then reign 3 years. His son Ghoṣa will be king 3 years. Next Vajramitra will be king 9 years.

> Bhāgavata will be king 32 years. His son Devabhūmi will reign 10 years. These 10 Śuṅga kings will enjoy this earth full 112 years. From them the earth will pass to the Kaṅvas.
>
> The minister Vasudeva, forcibly overthrowing the dissolute king Devabhūmi because of his youth, will become king among the Śuṅgas. He, the Kāṅvāyana, will be king 9 years. His son Bhūmimitra will reign 14 years. His son Nārāyaṅa will reign 12 years. His son Suśarman will reign 10 years. These are remembered as the Śuṅgabhṛtya Kāṅvāyana kings. These 4 Kaṅva Brāhmans will enjoy the earth; for 45 years they will enjoy this earth. They will have the neighbouring kings in subjection and will be righteous. In succession to them the earth will pass to Āndhras. [3]

Based on these regnal years, Tables 5.2 and 5.3 show the proposed chronology of Maurya and post-Maurya kings.

Table 5.2: The chronology of Maurya kings

King	Reign in years	Accepted Chronology [4]	Proposed Chronology
Chandragupta	24	324-300 BCE	919-895 BCE
Bindusāra	25	300-273 BCE	895-870 BCE
Aśoka	36	273-236 BCE	870-834 BCE
Kuṇāla	8	236-187 BCE	834-826 BCE
Bandhupālita	8		826-818 BCE
Daśona	7		818-811 BCE
Daśaratha	8		811-803 BCE
Samprati	9		803-794 BCE
Śāliśūka	13		794-781 BCE
Devadharman	7		781-774 BCE
Śatadhanvan	8		774-766 BCE
Bṛhadratha	70		766-696 BCE

Table 5.3: The chronology of post-Maurya kings

King	Reign in years	Accepted Chronology [5]	Proposed Chronology
Puṣyamitra (Śuṅga)	36	188-152 BCE	696-660 BCE
Agnimitra (Śuṅga)	8	152-144 BCE	660-652 BCE
Vasujyeṣṭha (Śuṅga)	7	144-137 BCE	652-645 BCE
Vasumitra (Śuṅga)	10	137-129 BCE	645-635 BCE
Andhraka (Śuṅga)	2	129-127 BCE	635-633 BCE
Pulindaka (Śuṅga)	3	127-124 BCE	633-630 BCE
Ghoṣa (Śuṅga)	3	124-121 BCE	630-627 BCE
Vajramitra (Śuṅga)	9	121-112 BCE	627-618 BCE
Bhāgavata (Śuṅga)	32	112-86 BCE	618-586 BCE
Devabhūmi (Śuṅga)	10	86-76 BCE	586-576 BCE
Vasudeva (Kaṇva)	9	76-67 BCE	576-567 BCE
Bhūmimitra (Kaṇva)	14	67-53 BCE	567-553 BCE
Nārāyaṇa (Kaṇva)	12	53-41 BCE	553-541 BCE
Suśarman (Kaṇva)	10	41-31 BCE	541-531 BCE

We should note here that Aśoka Maurya is called Aśoka the Great in history books, but the greatness attributed to him is because he is identified as Devānāmpriya Priyadarśī. In the light of the discovery that Kumāragupta-I was the real Devānāmpriya Priyadarśī, historians may want to reconsider whether Aśoka Maurya was great or not and whether Kumāragupta-I should be given the title of "the Great".

Some texts fix the date of ascension of Puṣyamitra at 187 BCE [6-7], in which case the dates from the accepted chronology in Table 5.3 can be moved down by one year to get the corresponding dates. The last Maurya king,

Bṛhadratha, was killed by his army general, Puṣyamitra Śuṅga, who established the Śuṅga dynasty. The last Śuṅga king was Devabhūmi, who was overthrown by his minister Vasudeva, who established the Kaṇva dynasty. The last king of the Kaṇva Dynasty was Suśarman, whose reign ended in 531 BCE, according to our calculations. What happened next is uncertain.

5.2 Āndhras

All Purāṇas are unanimous that the Āndhras came to power after overthrowing the last Kaṇva ruler, Suśarman. However, the Āndhras were a South Indian dynasty and there is no independent proof that they ruled from Magadha in North India. Another complication is that the kings listed in the Purāṇas as Āndhra kings call themselves Sātavāhana in their inscriptions. Not only that, they have not referred themselves as Āndhras even once in their inscriptions. Based on the literary evidence in the Purāṇas and inscriptional evidence, modern historians have combined them together as Āndhra-Sātavāhana kings. Indian tradition places the famous Sātavāhana king Gautamīputra Sātakarṇi in first century CE as the Śālivāhana Śaka had been instituted in the memory of him defeating the Śaka kings. Āndhras have been mentioned in the Aitareya Brāhmaṇa, which takes their antiquity to the second millennium BCE, as Brāhmaṇa texts were written before the time of the Buddha, who took birth in 13th century BCE as discussed in Chapter 3. Megasthenes, who came to India in the 3rd century BCE, said the following about the Āndhras:

> Next come the Andarae, a still more powerful race, which possesses numerous villages, and thirty towns

> defended by walls and towers, and which supplies its king with an army of 100,000 infantry, 2,000 cavalry, and 1,000 elephants. [8]

Obviously, the Āndhras were a powerful group of people in the 3rd century BCE. In the inscriptions of Devānāmpriya Priyadarśī or Kumāragupta-I, who ruled towards the end of 3rd century BCE and the beginning of 2nd century BCE, Āndhras have been grouped together with Pulinda in the 13th Rock Edict, while Chola, Pāṇḍya, Satiyaputra and Keralaputra are grouped together in the 2nd Rock Edict. Identification of Satiyaputra is not very clear, though clearly they were in South India as evident from their grouping with Chola, Pāṇḍya and Keralaputra. Satiyaputra may refer to Sātavāhanas as opined by some historians [9].

In the light of the information presented above, we can conclude that the Āndhras and the Sātavāhanas were totally different dynasties, which perhaps shared the last name, resulting in confusion about them belonging to the same dynasty. Chronologically, the Āndhras ruled several centuries earlier than the Sātavāhanas. Geographically, the Āndhras had their base in the eastern part of South India, while the Sātavāhanas had their base in the western part of South India. After the fall of the Kaṇvas, there remained no central authority in North India, while the Āndhras became the most prominent power in South India. Seeing that there was no paramount power in North India, the Persian Achaemenid emperor Darius I attacked the western borders of India around 515 BCE and added the areas around Indus valley from Gāndhara to modern day Karachi to his empire.

5.3 Ādi Śankarāchārya

It was in these troubled times that a man of unparalleled intellectual brilliance and spiritual vision rose to unite India culturally. We know him as Ādi Śankarāchārya, and what he achieved in merely 32 years of his life is almost superhuman. Born in 509 BCE (as per tradition) in Kaladi in present day Kerala, he travelled across all of India to spread the doctrine of Advaita Vedānta. He challenged the proponents of Mimānsā, Sāṅkhya and Buddhism for debate and defeated them. This is the true intellectual tradition of India. Hindus did not propagate the notion that all ideologies are true. Respect for one's worldview had to be earned. Ideologies were open to challenge and their proponents had to defend their ideologies in open debate. If they lost the debate, they were supposed to become the disciple of their challenger. Ādi Śaṅkarāchārya established four monasteries in the four corners of India to uphold and defend Hinduism. When he passed away in 477 BCE, he had already ensured that the light of the Vedas would continue to illuminate and guide generations of Hindus.

5.4 The Nāga Kingdoms

After the fall of the Kaṇvas, North India remained without a single paramount ruler till the formation of the Gupta Empire. According to the Purāṇas, a number of Nāga kings were ruling in North India before the rise of the Imperial Guptas:

> Hear also the future kings of Vidiśā. Bhogin, son of the Naga king Śeṣa, will be king, conqueror of his enemies' cities, a king who will exalt the Nāga family. Sadāchandra, and Chandrāṃśa who will be a second

> Nakhavant, then Dhanadharman, and Vaṅgara is remembered as the fourth. Then Bhūtinanda will reign in the Vaidiśa kingdom. … Nine Nāka kings will enjoy the city Champāvatī; and 7 Nāgas will enjoy the charming city Mathura. Kings born of the Gupta race will enjoy all these territories, namely, along the Ganges, Prayāga, Sāketa, and the Magadhas. [10]

According to this text Nāga kings were ruling at Vidiśā, Champāvatī and Mathura. As nine Nāga kings ruled at Champāvatī and seven Nāga kings ruled at Mathura before their defeat by Chandragupta-I and Samudragupta in the last quarter of the 4th century BCE, these Nāga kingdoms were established some time in the 5th century BCE. What is very interesting is that there was a Nāga king named Chandrāṃśa, who ruled at Vidiśā. He has been called a second Nakhavant in the Purāṇas. Nakha means nails and Nakhavant means a nail-cutter or a barber, as barbers also take care of nails in India [11]. In Chandrāṃśa, we then have the Xandrames of the Greek writers, who was ruling over the confederacy of Nāga kingdoms in North India at the time of Alexander's invasion. According to Greek writers, Xandrames was the son of a barber, who had usurped the kingdom [12-13]. Thus there is a striking match between the name and description of Xandrames by Greek writers with the name and description of Chandrāṃśa in the Purāṇas. At the time Nāga king Chandrāṃśa was ruling over parts of North India, a fearless king named Porus was guarding the western frontier of India.

Notes

1. Srivastava (2007): 123-130.
2. Jayaswal (1934): 14.
3. Pargiter (1913): 69-71.
4. Majumdar, Pusalker, and Majumdar (2001): 54-100.
5. Fergusson (1876): 716.
6. Olivelle (2006): 70-71.
7. Majumdar, Pusalker, and Majumdar (2001): 95-100.
8. McCrindle (1877): 138.
9. Sen (1999): 172.
10. Pargiter (1913): 72-73.
11. Sethna (1989): 183.
12. McCrindle (1893): 221-222.
13. Sethna (1989): 281-282.

"History is a pack of lies about events that never happened told by people who weren't there."

- George Santayana

6. Alexander's Defeat by Porus

The history of Alexander's invasion of India is known mainly through the Greek historians. There is no report from the Indian side regarding his battle with Porus. When there is information available from only one side, historians need to be extremely careful in arriving at conclusions as bias is inherent in such one-sided accounts. What happened during the battle been Alexander and Porus? Was Alexander really magnanimous after the battle? Have Greek historians lied regarding the outcome of this famous battle? Let us look carefully at and critically examine the available evidence.

6.1 Sources of Information

The information from Greek sources regarding the invasion of India by Alexander has been compiled together in "The Invasion of India by Alexander the Great" by John W. McCrindle, who relied on the following works for his compilation [1]:

- "The History of Alexander the Great" by Quintus Curtius Rufus
- "The History" by Diodoros the Sicilian

- "The Life of Alexander" in Plutarch's "Parallel Lives"
- "The Anabasis of Alexander" by Arrian of Nikomedeia
- "The Book of Macedonian History" compiled from the "Universal History of Trogus Pompeius" by Justinus Frontinus.

McCrindle gives the following information about the date of these Greek historians [2]. Nothing is known about the time at which Curtius lived, Diodoros was a contemporary of Julius Caesar and the Emperor Augustus (first century BCE), Plutarch lived towards the middle of the first century, Arrian was born towards the end of the first century, and Justinus cannot be later than the beginning of the fifth century.

6.2 The Encounter with Porus

India was a land of pious Brāhmaṇas, who did not care about material wealth. When Alexander met a Brāhmaṇa named Dandamis, Alexander was told by him that he desired nothing that was in Alexander's possession [3]. As Alexander moved towards India, the ruler of the region east of the Indus called variously Taxiles, Omphis and Mophis by Greek writers surrendered meekly, as described by Arrian, Curtius and Diodorus [4-8]. Taxiles ruled over a region between the rivers Indus and Hydaspes. The current name of Hydaspes is Jhelum and its ancient name was Vitastā.

Beyond Hydaspes a fearless warrior king named Porus was ready and waiting to defend his kingdom at any cost. Here is how Curtius describes the state of preparedness of Porus:

> In the van of his army he had posted 85 elephants of the greatest size and strength, and behind these 300 chariots and somewhere about 30,000 infantry, among whom were the archers, whose arrows, as already stated, were too ponderous to be readily discharged. He was himself mounted on an elephant which towered above all its fellows, while his armour, embellished with gold and silver, set off his supremely majestic person to great advantage. His courage matched his bodily vigour, and his wisdom was the utmost attainable in a rude community. [9]

We should note that Porus is always portrayed as courageous and wise by Greeks, while others are described as barbarians. It was not easy for Alexander to cross Hydaspes with his army under the constant watch of Porus. Alexander tried to fool Porus by manoeuvring his troops, but did not succeed completely [10]. He would give the impression of crossing the river but won't do it. Finally one night Alexander crosses Hydaspes with his army. The armies of Alexander and Porus charged against each other on the eastern side of the Hydaspes. Historians tell us that Porous lost and was captured. Plutarch has described the famous battle of the Hydaspes in the following words:

> When Poros was taken prisoner, Alexander asked him how he wished to be treated. "Like a king," answered Poros. When Alexander further asked if he had anything else to request, "Everything," rejoined Poros, "is comprised in the words, like a king." Alexander then not only reinstated Poros in his kingdom with the title of satrap, but added a large province to it, subduing the inhabitants whose form of government was the republican. This country, it is said, contained 15 tribes,

> 5000 considerable cities, and villages without number. [11]

We are told that Alexander was so impressed by the reply from Porus that he not only returned his kingdom but added to it. This must be the only instance in history when the loser ended up enlarging his kingdom. This is what we have read in history books. Is this what really happened that night? Let's take a critical look.

6.3 Did Alexander lose to Porus?

Marshal Georgi Zhukov was no ordinary man. He was the commander of the Russian Red Army, which pushed the Nazi army from Stalingrad all the way back to Berlin resulting in the collapse of the Nazi regime. He was the most successful Russian General during World War II and was known as the "man who did not lose a battle". When he was addressing the cadets of the Indian Military Academy, Dehradun in 1957, he said that Alexander had suffered an outright defeat during the Battle of Hydaspes. Here is an excerpt from the news report:

> In Zhukov's view, Alexander had suffered a greater setback in India than Napoleon in Russia. Napoleon had invaded Russia with 600,000 troops; of these only 30,000 survived, and of that number fewer than 1,000 were ever able to return to duty. So if Zhukov was comparing Alexander's campaign in India to Napoleon's disaster, the Macedonians and Greeks must have retreated in an equally ignominious fashion. Zhukov would know a fleeing force if he saw one; he had chased the German Army over 2000 km from Stalingrad to Berlin. [12]

Let me try to formulate the arguments in favour of Alexander's rout by Porus that would have prompted Zhukov to come to the shocking conclusion regarding the battle of the Hydaspes. Only when we critically analyze the pieces of evidence staring at us that we get to the truth.

6.3.1 If something is too good to be true, it probably is

We have heard about the magnanimity of Alexander after the battle of the Hydaspes. Arrian has described the outcome of this battle in the following words:

> Then Alexander, who was the first to speak, requested Poros to say how he wished to be treated. The report goes that Poros said in reply, "Treat me, O Alexander! as befits a king;" and that Alexander, being pleased with his answer, replied, "For mine own sake, O Poros! thou shalt be so treated, but do thou, in thine own behalf, ask for whatever boon thou pleasest," to which Poros replied that in what he had asked everything was included. Alexander was more delighted than ever with this rejoinder, and not only appointed Poros to govern his own Indians, but added to his original territory another of still greater extent. [13]

Isn't this too good to be true? Is there any other example in the entire history of humanity when the vanquished has not only been returned his kingdom, but more territory has been added to his kingdom?

6.3.2 Alexander was a cruel man

In the documentary series "Ancients behaving Badly" that aired in 2009 on The History Channel, a number of historical figures have been evaluated by historians and psychiatrists for being "goal driven killers" to "psychopathic murderers". These historical figures included Caligula, Attila the Hun, Julius Caesar, Alexander the Great, Nero, Hannibal, Genghis Khan, and Cleopatra. To make it to the list is proof enough that Alexander was not such a nice person that he is made out to be.

Alexander has been accused of conspiring to get his father killed in order to ascend the throne [14]. He killed many of his close subordinates unjustly. Hermolaus was a page to Alexander, who was executed for planning to kill him. According to Arrian, Hermolaus made the following accusations before his execution [15]:

> He then recounted all his acts of despotism, the illegal execution of Philotas, the still more illegal one of his father Parmenio and of others who were put to death at that time, the murder of Clitus in a fit of drunkenness, … He said that, being no longer able to bear these things, he wished to free both himself and other Macedonians.

Permenion was one of Alexander's most experienced and talented generals. Philotas was the eldest son of Permenion and commander of Companion cavalry. Both were executed for conspiring against Alexander. McCrindle has described the execution of Philotas in the following words:

> Here an event occurred which has left a dark stain on the character of Alexander. He was led to suspect that a conspiracy had been formed against his life by some of

> his principal officers, and among others by the son of Parmenion, Philotas, who held the most coveted post in the army, that of commander of the Companion Cavalry. It is certain that he was not an accomplice in the plot; but as he had been informed of its existence, and failed to give the king any warning of his danger, he was accused before the Macedonian army and condemned to death. He confessed under torture that his father, Parmenion, had formed a design against the king's life, and that he had himself joined the recent plot, lest his father, who was now an old man, might, before the plot was ripe, be snatched away by death from his command at Ekbatana, which placed the vast treasures deposited there at his disposal. This confession, wrung by torture when its agonies became insupportable, and obviously framed to meet the wishes of the questioners, was no proof of the guilt either of the father or the son. Parmenion was, nevertheless, on this worthless evidence condemned to death, and Alexander, whom he had so faithfully served, took care that the sentence should be executed before the news of his son's death, which he might seek to avenge, could reach his ears. Many other Macedonians were also at this time tried and put to death. [16]

It is clear that Alexander tortured and executed his military officers based on mere suspicion. The treatment of Bessus by Alexander is even more horrific. Arrian had described the inhuman treatment of Bessus by Alexander in the following words:

> Then Alexander gathered a conference of those who were then at hand, and led Bessus in before them. Having accused him of the betrayal of Darius, he ordered his nose and ears to be cut off, and that he

> should be taken to Ecbatana to be put to death there in the council of the Medes and Persians. [17]

Bessus was a Persian Satrap of Bactria who later declared himself the King of Kings of Persia. Alexander was a cruel dictator, who did not show mercy to this defeated king. Why would he be so magnanimous to Porus? He was so cruel and unethical that he even violated his own treaty by killing a number of people defending the town of Massaga after granting them immunity [18].

6.3.3 Alexander never showed kindness to anyone who opposed him

We are told that Alexander was very kind to Porus because he was very impressed by his bravery. However, Alexander had never shown any kindness to anyone who had opposed him. Here are some quotes to this effect:

> He took many other cities, and put to death all who offered resistance to his arms. [19]

> To resist Alexander was to incur his wrath regardless of your religious beliefs, cultural persuasion, or ethnic identity. Throughout his military operations, Alexander followed a policy of rewarding those who surrendered quickly and punishing severely those who resisted. The classic example of the latter was his destruction of the rebellious city of Thebes, one of the great cities of Hellenic civilization. [20]

> The cities along the Syrian coast submitted in like manner to Alexander himself, all but Tyre, which sent him a golden crown, but refused to admit him within her gates. For this temerity the city of merchant princes paid a dreadful penalty. Alexander, having captured it after a

> seven months' siege, burned it to the ground, and most of the inhabitants he either slew or sold into slavery. ... His merciless treatment of the vanquished darkly overshadows the glory of this memorable exploit." [21]

If Alexander was never kind to people resisting him, how could he suddenly become so kind to Porus?

6.3.4 An army has never refused to fight in history

We have been told by Greek historians that Alexander's army refused to fight after the battle with Porus, even though Alexander wanted to go ahead and invade the interior parts of India. Here is what Plutarch has said:

> The battle with Poros depressed the spirits of the Macedonians, and made them very unwilling to advance farther into India. For as it was with the utmost difficulty they had beaten him when the army he led amounted only to 20,000 infantry and 2000 cavalry, they now most resolutely opposed Alexander when he insisted that they should cross the Ganges. [22]

This was supposed to have been such a tough battle that Alexander's army could not take it anymore. But if we take the words of Arrian, who is supposed to be the most reliable among Greek historians, there was hardly any fight:

> The loss of the Indians in killed fell little short of 20,000 infantry and 3000 cavalry, and all their chariots were broken to pieces. Two sons of Poros fell in the battle, and also Spitakes, the chief of the Indians of that district.... On Alexander's side there fell about 80 of the 6000 infantry who had taken part in the first attack, 10 of the horse archers who first began the action, 20 of the

> companion cavalry, and 200 of the other cavalry. [23]

Does it look like a fight at all? This seems more like a cakewalk. If these are the real figures of the casualties on Alexander's side compared to Porus' side, Alexander's army should have been raring to go further. They did not and there is only one sane reason for that: because they could not. Never before in history and that includes not just up to Alexander's time, but up to our time, an army has refused to fight. In ancient times the soldiers would be executed and, now, they would be court-martialed. Armies have never had a choice in fighting anywhere in the world. It was always up to the ruler/leader to decide. We can therefore surmise that Greek historians cooked up an elaborate excuse to hide the real outcome of the battle.

6.3.5 Alexander was at a clear disadvantage

If Alexander and his army tried to cross the river Hydaspes, Porus was ready to attack them even before they could land on the other side. This is what Arrian has said [24]:

> Having appointed Philip, the son of Makhatas, satrap of the Indians of that district, he left a garrison in Taxila and those soldiers who were invalided, and then moved on towards the river Hydaspes - for he had learned that Porus with the whole of his army lay on the other side of that river resolved either to prevent him from making the passage or **to attack him when crossing**. [24]

On the other hand it was not easy to cross the Hydaspes at that time of the year, as told by Curtius [25]:

> The Macedonians were intimidated not only by the appearance of the enemy, but by the magnitude of the

> river to be crossed, which, spreading out to a width of no less than four stadia in a deep channel which nowhere opened a passage by fords, presented the aspect of a vast sea. Yet its rapidity did not diminish in proportion to its wider diffusion, but it rushed impetuously like a seething torrent compressed into a narrow bed by the closing in of its banks. Besides, at many points the presence of sunken rocks was revealed where the waves were driven back in eddies. The bank presented a still more formidable aspect, for, as far as the eye could see, it was covered with cavalry and infantry, in the midst of which, like so many massive structures, stood the huge elephants, which, being of set purpose provoked by their drivers, distressed the ear with their frightful roars. The enemy and the river both in their front, struck with sudden dismay the hearts of the Macedonians, disposed though they were to entertain good hopes, and knowing from experience against what fearful odds they had ere now contended. They could not believe that boats so unhandy could be steered to the bank or gain it in safety. [25]

The situation was even worse on the night of the crossing, as told by Plutarch:

> At last, upon a dark and stormy night, he took a part of the infantry and a choice body of cavalry, marched to a considerable distance from the enemy, and crossed over to an island of no great size. Here he was exposed with his army to the rage of a violent thunderstorm, amid which rain fell down in torrents, and though he saw some of his men struck dead with the lightning, he nevertheless advanced from the island and reached the furthermost bank of the river. The Hydaspes was now flooded by the rains, and its raging current had chosen a

> new channel of great width, down which a great body of water was carried. In fording this new bed, he could with difficulty keep his footing, as the bottom was very slippery and uneven. [26]

Under these circumstances, when crossing the Hydaspes was itself so fraught with danger, how was an army going to cross the river and then fight an enemy, who was ready on guard and determined not to let them cross the river? Alexander had crossed the river surreptitiously with a small battalion, but was already spotted during crossing. Most of his army had to cross right before the watchful eyes of Porus. Was he just going to sit and watch while they tried to cross the river? What were his archers for?

6.3.6 Alexander kept sending emissaries to Porus

If Porus was losing the battle, then why was Alexander so anxious to send emissary after emissary to ask Porus to stop fighting? This is exactly what Arrian has told us:

> When he found himself wounded he turned his elephant round and began to retire. Alexander, perceiving that he was a great man and valiant in fight, was anxious to save his life, and for this purpose sent to him first of all Taxiles the Indian. Taxiles, who was on horseback, approached as near the elephant which carried Poros as seemed safe, and entreated him, since it was no longer possible for him to flee, to stop his elephant and listen to the message he brought from Alexander. But Poros, on finding that the speaker was his old enemy Taxiles, turned round and prepared to smite him with his javelin; and he would probably have killed him had not Taxiles instantly put his horse to the gallop and got beyond the reach of Poros. But not even for this act did Alexander

> feel any resentment against Poros, **but sent to him messenger after messenger**, and last of all Meroes, an Indian, as he had learned that Poros and this Meroes were old friends. As soon as Poros heard the message which Meroes now brought just at a time when he was overpowered by thirst, he made his elephant halt and dismounted. Then, when he had taken a draught of water and felt revived, he requested Meroes to conduct him without delay to Alexander. [27]

It is hard to imagine why Alexander would have been anxious to save the life of Porus. It would only make sense if Alexander was losing the battle badly and was anxious to stop fighting.

6.3.7 Taxiles made no gains from the defeat of Porus

Taxiles had cooperated with Alexander in the hope of settling his score with Porus with whom he had enmity. However, for all his support, including taking part in the battle against Porus, Taxiles seems to have gained nothing in return from Alexander. He might have even been forced to give his daughter in marriage to Porus. Here is what Curtius has said:

> Designing now to make for the ocean with a thousand ships, he left Porus and Taxiles, the Indian kings who had been disagreeing and raking up old feuds, in friendly relations with each other, strengthened by a marriage alliance; and as they had done their utmost to help him forward with the building of his fleet, he confirmed each in his sovereignty. [28]

Alexander gave all the regions he had conquered to Porus. Taxiles was simply sent back to his capital with nothing to show for his loyalty. Here is what Arrian has said:

> In this manner he took seven-and-thirty cities, the smallest of which contained not fewer than 5000 inhabitants, while many contained upwards of 10,000. He took also a great many villages which were not less populous than the towns; and this country he gave to Poros to rule, and between him and Taxiles he effected a reconciliation. He then sent Taxiles home to his capital. [29]

6.3.8 Alexander did not avenge the loss of his dear horse Boukephalos in the battle

According to Diodoros, Alexander's horse Boukephala died in the battle with Porus:

> When the equipment of the fleet was finished, and 200 boats without hatches and 800 tenders had been got ready, he proceeded to give names to the cities which had been founded on the banks of the river, calling one Nikaia in commemoration of his victory, and the other Boukephala after his horse that perished in the battle with Poros. [30]

Curtius has also confirmed the death of Alexander's horse during the battle with Porus:

> Alexander pursued, but his horse being pierced with many wounds fainted under him, and sank to the ground, laying the king down gently rather than throwing him from his seat. [31]

McCrindle makes the following comments on this statement by Curtius [32]:

> Regarding this horse it seems worth recording that when caparisoned and armed for battle he would not suffer himself to be mounted by anyone but the king. It is also told of this horse that in the Indian war when Alexander, mounted upon him, and performing noble deeds of bravery, had with too little heed for his own safety entangled himself amid a battalion of the enemy, where he was on all sides assailed with darts, his horse was stabbed with deep wounds in the neck and sides. Ready to expire, and drained of nearly all his blood, he nevertheless bore back the king from the midst of his foes at a most rapid pace; and when he had conveyed him beyond reach of spears, he straightway dropped down, and having no further fear for his master's safety, he breathed his last as if with the consolation of human sensibility. Then King Alexander having gained the victory in this war, built a town on this spot, and in honour of his horse called it Bucephalon. [32]

Greek writers have tried to twist the outcome of the battle, but have clearly failed to hide it. It was Alexander who was surrounded by enemies from all sides and attacked. He was injured badly himself and his horse barely managed to take him to safety. This horse was very dear to Alexander. Arrian has told us that Alexander was going to kill all Ouxians when his horse Boukephalas went missing:

> This Boukephalas was never mounted by anyone except Alexander only, for he disdained all other riders. He was of uncommon size and of generous mettle. He had by way of a distinguishing mark the head of an ox impressed upon him, and some say that from this

> circumstance he got his name. But others say that though he was black, he had on his forehead a white mark which bore a close resemblance to the brow of an ox. In the country of the Ouxians this horse disappeared from Alexander, who sent a proclamation through the land that he would kill all the Ouxians if they did not bring him his horse, and brought back he was immediately after the proclamation had been issued - so great was Alexander's attachment to his favourite, and so great was the fear of Alexander which prevailed among the barbarians. [33]

If Porus had lost the battle in which Alexander's horse had died, there was no way Alexander would have left Porus alive. It follows then that it was Alexander who was sending messengers after messengers to Porus to stop the battle.

6.3.9 Alexander did not return by the land route

When Alexander had decided that he was not going any further, he did not return by the land route he had taken to come to India. A victor would have gone back celebrating. Instead he went back through unchartered territory endangering the lives of his army. The reason is clear. He was not allowed to go back using the land route by Porus. Porus was not only a great warrior, but also a very strategic thinker. He figured out that if he let Alexander go back across the Hydaspes, Alexander was simply going to strengthen his army and come back to avenge his defeat. Instead, Porus gave him the only option, which was certain to diminish if not ruin his power.

6.3.10 Alexander took an unknown perilous route back through the Hydaspes and the Indus rivers to sea

Alexander had to go back by sailing through Hydaspes first and then through the Indus river. It took his army months to cut trees and build the fleet for this purpose. Here is what Greek writer Strabo has written:

> Between the Hydaspes and Akesines is the country of Poros – an extensive and fertile district containing somewhere about 300 cities. Here in the neighbourhood of the Emodoi mountains is the forest where Alexander cut a great quantity of pine, fir, cedar and various other trees fit for shipbuilding. This timber he brought down the Hydaspes, and with it constructed a fleet on that river .... [34]

Why would Alexander's army take up so much work, when they were too tired to fight according to the story made up to justify not going any further into India? Why would they take a perilous route if Alexander had won the battle with Porus? Is it conceivable that the greatest military strategist of all times, who had travelled thousands of miles to reach the land of Porus, did not know what awaited him a few miles down the river if he took a journey through Hydaspes? Clearly, Alexander was left with no choice by Porus. As Porus had lost his son in the battle, obviously he was not in a charitable mood. Alexander had to take this perilous route knowing the danger fully well. Here is what had happened at the confluence of the Hydaspes and Indus rivers according to Curtius:

> But the meeting of the rivers makes the waters swell in great billows like those of the ocean, and the navigable way is compressed into a narrow channel by extensive

> mud-banks kept continually shifting by the force of the confluent waters. When the waves, therefore, in thick succession dashed against the vessels, beating both on their prows and sides, the sailors were obliged to take in sail; but partly from their own flurry, and partly from the force of the currents, they were unable to execute their orders in time, and before the eyes of all two of the large ships were engulphed in the stream. The smaller craft, however, though they also were unmanageable, were driven on shore without sustaining injury. The ship which had the king himself on board was caught in eddies of the greatest violence, and by their force was irresistibly driven athwart and whirled onward without answering the helm. He had already stripped off his clothes preparatory to throwing himself into the river, while his friends were swimming about not far off ready to pick him up, but as it was evident that the danger was about equal whether he threw himself into the water or remained on board, the boatmen vied with each other in stretching to their oars, and made every exertion possible for human beings to force their vessel through the raging surges. It then seemed as though the waves were being cloven asunder, and as though the whirling eddies were retreating, and the ship was thus at length rescued from their grasp. It did not, however, gain the shore in safety, but was stranded on the nearest shallows. One would suppose that a war had been waged against the river. [35]

Things went from bad to worse for Alexander's army as they continued further. They had to fight for their supplies and there seemed no end to their misery. Curtius continues with the following description:

> New enemies were forever springing up with arms ever new, and though they put them all to rout and flight, what reward awaited them? What but mists and darkness and unbroken night hovering over the abyss of ocean? What but a sea teeming with multitudes of frightful monsters-stagnating waters in which expiring nature has given way in despair?
>
> The king, troubled not by any fears for himself, but by the anxiety of the soldiers about their safety, called them together, and pointed out to them that those of whom they were afraid were weak and unwarlike; that after the conquest of these tribes there was nothing in their way, once they had traversed the distance now between them and the ocean, to prevent their coming to the end of the world, which would be also the end of their labours; that he had given way to their fears of the Ganges and of the numerous tribes beyond that river, and turned his arms to a quarter where the glory would be equal but the hazard less; that they were already in sight of the ocean, and were already fanned by breezes from the sea. They should not then grudge him the glory to which he aspired. They would overpass the limits reached by Hercules and Father Bacchus, and thus at a small cost bestow upon their king an immortality of fame. They should permit him to return from India with honour, and not to escape from it like a fugitive. [36]

There we have it as explicit as it can get. Alexander was himself begging his army to let him return with honour and not return like a fugitive. If this is not the admission of defeat in the battle, what else would be?

6.3.11 Alexander lost most of his army on the way back

When Alexander finally reached the sea, he divided his army and one division took the sea route while the rest followed the land route close to the sea through the desert of Gedrosia. Strabo has described this part of the journey in the following words:

> Having made three divisions of his army, he advanced himself with one of them through Gedrosia, keeping at most a distance from the sea of 500 stadia, that he might make preparations along the coast for the benefit of his fleet. He was frequently in close proximity to the sea, although the beach was impracticable and rugged. The second division he sent on before him, under Krateros, through the interior, that he might reduce Ariane, while advancing to the places to which Alexander himself was directing his march. The fleet he entrusted to Nearchos and Onesikritos, the pilot-in-chief, instructing them to take up convenient positions as they followed him, and to sail along the coast parallel to his line of march. Nearchos relates that while Alexander was marching away from India, he himself, in Autumn, about the time when the Pleiades rise after sunset, began his voyage, even though the winds were contrary, because the barbarians were attacking his troops and trying to drive them out of the country. They had waxed bold after the king's departure, and were bent on asserting their liberty. Krateros again settling out from the Hydaspes went through the country of the Arachotians and Drangians into Karmania. But Alexander suffered sorely all throughout his march, as his road lay through a miserably barren country. He was equally unfortunate in the matter of provisions, which were not only brought from a distance, but brought so seldom and in such small

quantities, that the army suffered greatly from hunger, while the beasts of burden broke down, and the baggage was abandoned both on the march and in the camp. The army was indebted for its salvation to the dates and edible pith of the palm trees. Nearchos says that Alexander, being impressed with the current report that Semiramis had effected her escape from India with about twenty men and Cyrus with about seven, was ambitious, though aware of the difficulties and dangers of the enterprise, to conduct his large army through the same country in safety and triumphantly. In addition to the want of provisions, the scorching heat and the depth of the sand and its burning heat were hard to bear. In some places, too, there were high ridges of sand, so that, besides the difficulty of lifting the legs as out of a deep hole, there were ascents and descents. It was necessary also, on account of the watering places, to make long marches of 200, 400, and even at times of 600 stadia, and generally by night. The camp was pitched at a distance from the wells, and frequently 30 stadia away from them, to prevent the soldiers from drinking to excess from thirst; for many of them threw themselves into the water in their armour, drank of it, and sank below the surface till life was extinct, when their bodies became swollen, and corrupted the shallow waters of the cisterns. Others exhausted by thirst lay exposed to the sun in the middle of the road. Their legs and arms twitched convulsively, and they died like persons seized with cold and shivering. Some turned aside from the road to indulge in sleep, overcome with drowsiness and fatigue. Being thus left behind, some of them lost their way and perished from utter destitution and the heat, while others escaped with their lives after direful sufferings. A winter torrent again, which burst upon

> them in the night time, destroyed many lives and a great quantity of baggage, besides sweeping away a considerable portion of the royal equipage. The guides through ignorance deviated so far into the interior that the sea was no longer in view. [37]

Arrian has described the misery of Alexander's army through the Gedrosian desert in the following words:

> The soldiers destroyed many of the beasts of burden of their own accord. For when their provisions ran short they came together and killed most of the horses and mules. They ate the flesh of these animals, which they professed had died of thirst and perished from the heat. No one cared to look very narrowly into the exact nature of what was doing, both because of the prevailing distress and also because all were alike implicated in the same offence. Alexander himself was not unaware of what was going on, but he saw that the remedy for the existing state of things was to pretend ignorance of it rather than permit it as a matter that lay within his cognizance. It was therefore no longer easy to convey the soldiers labouring under sickness, nor others who had fallen behind on the march from exhaustion. This arose not only from the want of beasts of burden, but also because the men themselves took to destroying the waggons when they could no longer drag them forward owing to the deepness of the sand. They had done this even in the early stages of the march, because for the sake of the waggons they had to go not by the shortest roads, but those easiest for carriages. Thus some were left behind on the road from sickness, others from fatigue or the effects of the heat or intolerable thirst, while there were none who could take them forward or remain to tend them in their sickness. For the army

> marched on apace, and in the anxiety for its safety as a whole the care of individuals was of necessity disregarded. As they generally made their marches by night, some of the men were overcome by sleep on the way, but on awaking afterwards those who still had some strength left followed close on the track of the army, and a few out of many saved their lives by overtaking it. The majority perished in the sand like shipwrecked men at sea. [38]

According to Plutarch, Alexander lost more than three fourths of his army on the way back from India:

> He himself, returning by land with the army, marched through the country of the Oreitai, where he was reduced to the sorest straits from the scarcity of provisions, and lost such numbers of men that he hardly brought back from India the fourth part of his military force, though he entered it with 120,000 foot and 15,000 horse. Many perished from malignant distempers, wretched food, and scorching heat, but most from sheer hunger, for their march lay through an uncultivated region, inhabited only by some miserable savages, the owners of a small and inferior breed of sheep, accustomed to feed on sea-fish, which gave to their flesh a rank and disagreeable flavour. [39]

No military commander would willingly let this happen to his army. That Alexander, who is considered to be the greatest military commander till his time and probably even till our time by many, would let this happen to his army is inconceivable. The only sensible explanation for this turn of events is his defeat at the hands of Porus.

6.3.12 Alexander's historians are liars

The arguments presented so far clearly point to the possibility that Greek historians have lied regarding the outcome of the battle of the Hydaspes. In fact, one of their own, Strabo (II.I.9) has accused Greek writers of being liars:

> Generally speaking, the men who hitherto have written on the affairs of India, were a set of liars. Deimachus holds the first place in the list, Megasthenes comes next, while Onesicritus and Nearchus, with others of the same class, manage to stammer out a few words [of truth]. [40]

McCrindle makes the following remarks about Plutarch:

> This seems an almost inexcusable mistake on Plutarch's part-his conducting Alexander as far as the Ganges! The author of the Periplus made the same egregious blunder. It is possible, however, to put a different construction on the expressions used by Plutarch, and to suppose that he wrote so carelessly that he did not mean what his words seem to imply. [41]

It is clear from these passages that Greek historians were not very objective and have turned Alexander's defeat into a fictitious tale of his magnanimity.

6.3.13 Alexander fought under Porus beyond Hydaspes

We may be asked how and whether Alexander continued his campaign further before deciding to return if he had indeed lost to Porus. Greek writers claim that Alexander subdued a number of kingdoms after his victory over Porus and Porus helped him as a subordinate during these campaigns [42]. The explanation is simple. It was Alexander who fought under the command of Porus, who used this opportunity to expand his territory further. Alexander had to fight with part of his army, while the rest of his army was busy cutting trees and building a fleet for their return journey. This is affirmed by what happened after the campaigns, according to Arrian:

> He then assembled the companions and all the ambassadors of the Indians who had come to him, and in their presence appointed Poros king of all the Indian territories already subjugated - seven nations in all, containing more than 2000 cities. [43]

Why would Porus be made the king of all Indian territories? Greek writers have lied about the result of the battle of the Hydaspes, but they could not conceal the real outcome of the battle, which was the enlargement of the territories ruled by Porus. Now that we have presented arguments in the favor of Porus winning the battle of the Hydaspes, it is up to the historians to decide what to believe: a series of extraordinary events or a likely set of events consistent with Alexander's character. A warrior of indomitable courage named Porus, who fought fearlessly to save his kingdom from being plundered by Alexander's army, deserves his respectful place in the annals of history. Should he be denied justice and honor just because he didn't employ historians to write the saga of his bravery?

The fearless act of Porus was followed by a series of brave response by rulers, who called themselves Vikramāditya. The Vikrama era was constituted in the name of one of those Vikramādityas.

Notes:

1. McCrindle (1893): 8-9.
2. McCrindle (1893): 9-15.
3. McCrindle (1893): 387.
4. McCrindle (1893): 58-59.
5. McCrindle (1893): 83.
6. McCrindle (1893): 92.
7. McCrindle (1893): 201-202.
8. McCrindle (1893): 273.
9. McCrindle (1893): 202-204.
10. McCrindle (1893): 94-99.
11. McCrindle (1893): 307-309.
12. http://in.rbth.com/blogs/2013/05/27/marshal_zhukov_on_alexanders_failed_india_invasion_25383.html.
13. McCrindle (1893): 109.
14. Anson (2013): 79.
15. Chinnock (1884): 232.
16. McCrindle (1893): 37-38.
17. Chinnock (1884): 217.
18. McCrindle (1893): 269-270.
19. McCrindle (1893): 271.
20. Anson (2013): 124.
21. McCrindle (1893): 26-27.
22. McCrindle (1893): 310.
23. McCrindle (1893): 107-108.
24. McCrindle (1893): 92.
25. McCrindle (1893): 204.
26. McCrindle (1893): 307.
27. McCrindle (1893): 108-109.

28. McCrindle (1893): 231.
29. McCrindle (1893): 112.
30. McCrindle (1893): 284.
31. McCrindle (1893): 212.
32. McCrindle (1893): 212.
33. McCrindle (1893): 110-111.
34. McCrindle (1901): 35-36.
35. McCrindle (1893): 233-234.
36. McCrindle (1893): 234-235.
37. McCrindle (1901): 83-85.
38. McCrindle (1893): 174.
39. McCrindle (1893): 316.
40. Hamilton (1892): 108-109.
41. McCrindle (1893): 310, footnote.
42. McCrindle (1893): 279-282.
43. McCrindle (1893): 133.

"When the will defies fear, when duty throws the gauntlet down to fate, when honor scorns to compromise with death - that is heroism."

- Robert Green Ingersoll

7. The Age of Vikramādityas

In the fourth century BCE, North India was divided into many small kingdoms. However, India was culturally united and its people took extreme pride in belonging to the land they considered coveted by the Gods. Nāgas were a powerful force in North India, while Vākāṭakas ruled from South India. A marriage alliance took place between the Nāgas and the Vākāṭakas to present a united front in response to the impending invasion by Alexander.

The Nāgas were one of the original inhabitants of India. A lot of confusion exists regarding the history of the Nāgas. Just like the stories of Vikramāditya, cosmological, astronomical and the apparent meaning of Nāga have become enmeshed with the historical stories of the Nāgas. This web of fact and myths needs to be carefully disentangled to uncover the real history of the Nāgas.

The apparent meaning of Nāga is a cobra, and this has prompted the depiction of the Nāgas as cobras. However, the Nāgas were real people, and it is obvious from the marriage of the Nāga princesses with Vākāṭaka and Gupta rulers. The depiction of human Nāgas as cobras has given rise to the story of shape-shifting cobras in the popular imagination. Ichchhādhārī Nāgas, as they are called, have the ability to change to human form from the cobra form and vice-versa. These shape-shifting Nāgas are supposed to guard fabulous treasures, which probably has its origin in the Nāga kings amassing huge fortunes.

Another popular myth based on this depiction is that of Viṣakanyās, i.e. poison-girls. Viṣakanyās were very pretty girls, who were administered poison since childhood in slowly increasing quantities. They were so full of venom by the time they became adult that if they kissed someone, that person would die immediately. They were sent to rival kings to present the kiss of death.

Many Nāga kings were staunch devotees of Lord Śiva. We find the following information in the Chammak copper plate inscription of the Vākāṭaka king Pravarasena II:

> Who was the son of the Mahārāja of the Vākāṭakas, the illustrious Rudrasena (I), who was an excessively devout devotee of (the god) Svāmī-Mahābhairava; who was the daughter's son of the illustrious Bhavanāga, the Mahārāja of the Bhāraśivas, whose royal line owed its origin to the great satisfaction of (the god) Śiva, (caused) by (their) carrying a liṅga of Śiva placed as a load upon (their) shoulders, (and) who were besprinkled on the forehead with the pure water of (the) river Bhāgīrathī that had been obtained by (their) valour, and (who) performed ablutions after the celebration of ten asvamedha sacrifices; ... [1]

According to this inscription, Bhāraśiva Nāgas received their name due to carrying a liṅga of Śiva on their shoulders and their kings had performed ten Aśvamedha sacrifices on the banks of the Ganges. It seems reasonable to assume that the famous Daśaśvamedha Ghāṭa in Varanasi received its name from the performance of ten Aśvamedha sacrifices by Bhāraśiva Nāga kings.

A number of Nāga kings were ruling in North India before the rise of the Imperial Guptas, according to the Purāṇas:

> Hear also the future kings of Vidiśā. Bhogin, son of the Naga king Śeṣa, will be king, conqueror of his enemies' cities, a king who will exalt the Nāga family. Sadāchandra, and Chandrāṃśa who will be a second Nakhavant, then Dhanadharman, and Vaṅgara is remembered as the fourth. Then Bhūtinanda will reign in the Vaidiśa kingdom. … Nine Nāka kings will enjoy the city Champāvatī; and 7 Nāgas will enjoy the charming city Mathura. Kings born of the Gupta race will enjoy all these territories, namely, along the Ganges, Prayāga, Sāketa, and the Magadhas. [2]

The above text shows that Vidiśā, Champāvatī and Mathurā were three centres of Nāga power. Elsewhere in the Purāṇas, Padmāvatī and Kāntipurī are also described as seats of Nāga power. Mathurā is a well known city in Uttar Pradesh. Vidisha is a city in Madhya Pradesh about 60 km northeast of Bhopal, the capital city of Madhya Pradesh. During the medieval times, this city was known as Bhilsa. Champāvatī is the same as Padmāvatī [3]. Alexander Cunningham had wrongly identified Padmāvatī with Narwar near Gwalior, but was corrected by M.B. Garde, who identified Padmāvatī with Pawaya, also known as Padam Pawaya [4]. Pawaya is about 70 km south of Gwalior in Madhya Pradesh. Kantipurī is the village of Kotwal, about 40 km north of Gwalior [5]. Thus the four major centres of the Nāga power -- Vidiśā, Padmāvatī (Champāvatī), Kāntipurī and Mathura -- covered a large part of North India, and the marriage of the daughter of Bhāraśiva Nāga king Bhavanāga with Vākāṭaka crown prince Gautamīputra from Deccan around 330 BCE resulted in a formidable confederation to take on the impending invasion of India by Alexander.

Further east, the Guptas were ruling in Magadha south of the Ganges, while a powerful Vajji confederation including Lichchhavis was ruling north of the Ganges from Vaiśālī. A second marriage alliance took place between the Guptas and the Lichchhavis to present a second wall of defence.

The first known ruler of the Imperial Gupta dynasty was Gupta, who was followed by Ghaṭotkachagupta. Around 330 BCE, Chandragupta-I, son of Ghaṭotkachagupta, was married to the Lichchhavi princess Kumāradevī, which greatly enhanced the power and prestige of the Guptas. It was this marriage alliance that changed the fortunes of the Guptas. Kumāradevī gave birth to Samudragupta, who later united a large part of India under one rule and was the first emperor to take the title of Vikramāditya. Chandragupta-I was a young man when the forces of Alexander reached the borders of India in 327 BCE. He enlisted himself in Alexander's army and encouraged fellow Indians to rebel against Alexander [6].

Further light on the meeting of Chandragupta with Alexander is thrown by the Greek classical writer Plutarch:

> Alexander at first in vexation and rage withdrew to his tent, and shutting himself up lay there feeling no gratitude towards those who had thwarted his purpose of

> crossing the Ganges; but regarding a retreat as tantamount to a confession of defeat. But being swayed by the persuasions of his friends, and the entreaties of his soldiers who stood weeping and lamenting at the door of his tent, he at last relented, and prepared to retreat. He first, however, contrived many unfair devices to exalt his fame among the natives, as, for instance, causing arms for men and stalls and bridles for horses to be made much beyond the usual size, and these he left scattered about. He also erected altars for the gods which the kings of the Praisiai even to the present day hold in veneration, crossing the river to offer sacrifices upon them in the Hellenic fashion. Androkottos himself, who was then but a youth, saw Alexander himself, and afterwards used to declare that Alexander could easily have taken possession of the whole country since the king was hated and despised by his subjects for the wickedness of his disposition and the meanness of his origin. [7]

After Alexander's devastating defeat at the hands of Porus, Chandragupta returned from the border. Now he was even more resolved to bring India under a unifying force to thwart any future invasion. He started to build his forces for this purpose. He received assistance from his in-laws, who united under his banner. To the west, the confederation of the Nāgas and the Vākāṭakas posed a formidable challenge and Chandragupta had to wait a while for an opportune moment. Under the leadership of his father Ghaṭotkachagupta, he started to slowly expand his territory and consolidate his forces with the help of the Vajji confederation of which his in-laws Lichchhavis were an important part.

Vajji or Vṛji region was the area east of the river Gaṇḍaka, west of the river Koshi, north of the Ganges and south of Nepal. The Vajji state was a republic consisting of a confederacy of eight clans. Four major clans of this confederacy were Videha, Lichchhavi, Jñātrika and Vṛji. The names of other four clans are lost to us. The capital of Vajji republic was located at Vaiśālī, which is present day Basarh in the state of Bihar, about 35 km southwest of Muzaffarpur. Videha was an ancient kingdom, with its capital at Mithilā. The kings of Videha kept the title of Janak.

The Vajji confederation was formed after the fall of the kingdom of Videha. Around 330 BCE, Chandragupta-I, son of Ghaṭotkachagupta, was married to the Lichchhavi princess Kumāradevī in response to the impending invasion by Alexander, and the marriage alliance between the Nāgas and Vākāṭakas. When the Imperial Guptas became the paramount power of India, Lichchhavis were emboldened to venture further north to Nepal. In the light of the chronology developed in this book, the history of Nepal will also need to undergo serious revision as the Lichchhavis came to Nepal six centuries before what is believed currently. The marriage alliance between the Guptas and Lichchhavis proved to be of great benefit to both and from this marriage alliance was born one of the greatest emperors of India and the first historical emperor to assume the title of Vikramāditya.

7.1 Samudragupta the Great

During the time of consolidation of Gupta power, Chandragupta-I paid special attention in grooming

Samudragupta to be a formidable warrior. Finally, around 310 BCE, the opportunity arrived for which the Guptas were waiting for a long time. With the death of the Vākāṭaka king Pravarasena-I in 310 BCE, there was a struggle for the throne. Vākāṭaka power was divided and a separate branch of Vākāṭakas was established at Vatsagulma. The Nāgas could not remain neutral in this fight for succession among the Vākāṭakas, and the Nāga unity was broken. Chandragupta-I and Samudragupta challenged the Nāgas in a series of rapid attacks. They came down heavily on the Nāga kings and exterminated them before they had a chance to regroup. To celebrate this grand achievement, Chandragupta-I was handed over the reigns of the now expanded Gupta kingdom by his overjoyed father Ghaṭotkachagupta in 309 BCE. The coronation of Chandragupta-I became the zero point for counting the dates of the Gupta era. By 305 BCE, Chandragupta-I had extended his empire to the borders of India. This is the time, Seleucus, who was one of the commanders under Alexander and had taken over part of Alexander's empire, attacked India to seek revenge for Alexander's defeat. However, Seleucus was defeated after a prolonged war and made a pact by offering his daughter in marriage to Samudragupta, who was of marriageable age at that time. Seleucus also ceded territories to Chandragupta-I that extended his empire all the way to present day Afghanistan. In return, Seleucus received 500 war elephants from Chandragupta-I, which helped him in defeating his rivals. Greek historian Plutarch has given the following account of the meeting of Chandragupta and Seleucus:

> The battle with Poros depressed the spirits of the Macedonians, and made them very unwilling to advance farther into India. For as it was with the utmost difficulty they had beaten him when the army he led amounted only to 20,000 infantry and 2000 cavalry, they now most resolutely opposed Alexander when he insisted that they should cross the Ganges. This river, they heard, had a breadth of two-and-thirty stadia, and a depth of 100 fathoms, while its farther banks were covered all over with armed men, horses, and elephants. For the kings of the Gandaritai and the Praisiai were reported to be waiting for him with an army of 80,000 horse, 200,000 foot, 8000 war chariots, and 6000 fighting elephants. Nor was this any exaggeration, for not long afterwards Androkottos, who had by that time mounted the throne, presented Seleukos with 500 elephants, and overran and subdued the whole of India with an army of 600,000 men. [8]

Greek classical writer Strabo has given the following account of the pact between Chandragupta and Seleucus:

> The Indus runs in a parallel course along the breadth of these regions. The Indians possess partly some of the countries lying along Indus, but these belonged formerly to the Persians. Alexander took them away from the Arianoi and established in them colonies of his own. Seleukos Nikator gave them to Sandrokottus in concluding a marriage alliance, and received in exchange 500 elephants. [9]

We need to keep in mind here that Greek writers do not specify who was married to whom. Since Seleucus lost the war, it is assumed that he offered his daughter in marriage to conclude the alliance. Looking at this evidence in conjunction with the proud declaration of Samudragupta in the Eran Stone inscription, we realize that the daughter of Seleucus was married to Samudragupta.

In the Eran Stone Inscription, Samudragupta claims to have earned his wife using his prowess:

> (L. 9.)— ... there was Samudragupta, equal to (the gods) Dhanada and Antaka in (respectively) pleasure and anger; . . . by policy; (and) [by whom] the whole tribe of kings upon the earth was [overthrown] and reduced to the loss of the wealth of their sovereignty; ...
> (L. 17.)— [By whom] there was married a virtuous and faithful wife, whose dower was provided by (his) manliness and prowess; who was possessed of an abundance of [elephants] and horses and money and grain; who delighted in the houses of . . . ; (and) who went about in the company of many sons and sons' sons; ... [10]

The exact words used in the inscription are "pauruṣa-parākrama-datta-śulkā" meaning whose nuptial gift was paid by manliness and prowess. Samudragupta's wife was named Dattadevī. The first part of the name "Datta" means given, as in given by her father due to defeat in war. The second part Devī is simply an honorific for a lady. Thus, Dattadevī was not her name before marriage, but given after marriage, according to the circumstances. We are fortunate to have received a very good account of the heroic deeds of the great emperor Samudragupta in the Allahabad Stone Pillar inscription [11]. This inscription gives the details of the extent of the biggest empire India had seen up to that point in time. In current history books, the Mauryan Empire is shown as being larger than the empire of the Imperial Guptas. This is based on the identification of Devānāmpriya Priyadarśī with Aśoka Maurya and making the boundaries of the Mauryan Empire based on the locations of the inscriptions of Devānāmpriya Priyadarśī and the subjects mentioned in the inscriptions. As Kumāragupta-I was the real Devānāmpriya Priyadarśī, extent of currently accepted Mauryan empire is actually the extent of Imperial Gupta empire.

Samudragupta was a great Hindu emperor, who embodied all the good qualities of the legendary king Vikramāditya. He was full of compassion, had a tender heart, and was a great benefactor of the poor and the helpless. He was kindness personified. He was not only a great warrior, but also possessed a sharp and polished intellect. He was an accomplished musician and a poet of note.

Samudragupta was the first emperor to take the title of Vikramāditya. It is proven from the fact that on one of his coins his title is given as Śrī Vikrama [12]. Samudragupta was a very able administrator, and opted for different policies for different kingdoms. Some of them, like the Nāgas, were exterminated and their kingdoms were made part of the empire, while others, such as Vākāṭakas, were allowed to rule as long as they were subordinate to him.

7.2 The Vākāṭakas

The Vākāṭakas were a powerful force in the south, and as long as they were united and their alliance with the Nāgas was intact, the Imperial Guptas were not in a position to subdue them. The founder of the Vākāṭaka dynasty was Vindhyaśakti. Literary and epigraphic data suggest that Vindhyaśakti was ruling from the region of Vidarbha in

Maharashtra. The Vākāṭakas rapidly rose in power under the rule of Pravarasena-I, son of Vindhyaśakti. He performed a number of Vedic sacrifices and assumed the title of Samrāṭa -- a term used in ancient India to signify a universal monarch. Pravarasena-I cemented an alliance with the powerful Nāga king Bhavanāga by getting his son Gautamiputra married to the daughter of Bhavanāga in circa 330 BCE. Gautamiputra predeceased his father. Pravarasena-I ruled for sixty years and after his death in 310 BCE, there was a battle for succession. The Vākāṭaka empire broke apart and Rudrasena-I, grandson of Pravarasena-I, ascended the throne of the main branch, while Sarvasena, second son of Pravarasena-I, founded the Vatsagulma branch. Pravarasena-I had four sons, and the other two sons may have held parts of the Vākāṭaka Empire. At this time, the unity of Nāga alliance also fell apart, as they took sides in the family feud of the Vākāṭakas. This provided the opportunity to the Imperial Guptas to quickly sweep upon the unsuspecting Nāgas and carry on with the mission of establishing a mighty empire, the like of which India had not seen before. As Chandragupta-I and Samudragupta continued on their victorious march, the divided Vākāṭakas were in no position to engage in a direct fight with the Imperial Guptas and simply accepted their sovereignty. It is for this reason that no Vākāṭaka king after Pravarasena-I assumed the title of Samrāṭa. Rudrasena-I was succeeded by his son Prithvīsena-I, who was succeeded by his son Rudrasena II. Rudrasena II was married to Prabhāvatīguptā, daughter of Imperial Gupta emperor Chandragupta-II, who himself was married to Kuberanāgā, a Nāga princess. Thus, once sovereignty of the Imperial Guptas was established over the Vākāṭakas and the Nāgas, friendly relations followed by the consummation of marriage alliances between them. With the foregoing in mind, the revised chronology of the Imperial Guptas and the Vākāṭakas is shown in Tables 7.1 and 7.2.

Table 7.1: New Chronology of Imperial Guptas

Gupta Monarch	**Regnal years**	**Current Timeline [13]**	**Proposed Timeline**
Chandragupta-I	1-31	319-350 CE	309-294 BCE
Samudragupta	31-57	350-376 CE	294-252 BCE
Chandragupta-II	57-96	376-415 CE	252-213 BCE
Kumāragupta-I	96-128	415-447 CE	213-173 BCE
Ghatotkachagupta	129-136	448-455 CE	
Skandagupta	137-148	456-467 CE	172-161 BCE
Narasiṃhagupta	148-155	467-474 CE	161-154 BCE
Kumāragupta-II	155-157	474-476 CE	154-152 BCE
Budhagupta	158-169	477-488 CE	151-140 BCE
Vainyagupta II	189	506 CE	120 BCE
Viṣṇugupta	196	515 CE	113 BCE

The data on regnal years in Table 7.1 has been calculated from the dynastic chart given in the paper "Later Gupta History: Inscriptions, Coins and Historical Ideology" by Michael Willis [13]. Using these regnal years with the start date of 309 BCE for Imperial Gupta era will imply that Chandragupta-I ruled from 309-278 BCE and Samudragupta ruled from 278-252 BCE.

Table 7.2: New Chronology of Vākāṭakas

Vākāṭaka King	**Accepted Date [14]**	**Proposed Date**
Vindhyaśakti I	250 CE	390 BCE
Pravarasena I	270 CE	370 BCE
Main branch		
Rudrasena I	330 CE	310 BCE
Prithvīsena I	350 CE	290 BCE
Rudrasena II	400 CE	240 BCE
Divākarasena	405 CE	235 BCE
Pravarasena II	420 CE	220 BCE
Narendrasena	450 CE	190 BCE
Prithvīsena II	470 CE	170 BCE
Vatsagulma branch		
Sarvasena	330 CE	310 BCE
Vindhyaśakti II	355 CE	285 BCE
Pravarasena II	400 CE	240 BCE
Son (unnamed)	410 CE	240 BCE
Devasena	450 CE	190 BCE
Harisena	475 CE	165 BCE
Son (unnamed)	500 CE	140 BCE

Assuming Chandragupta-I to be 20-years-old when he married Kumāradevī in 330 BCE, Chandragupta-I would be 41-years-old when he ascended the throne in 309 BCE. This seems fine and appropriate for his age. The problem is with the duration of his reign. If Chandragupta-I ruled for 31 years till 278 BCE, he would be 72-years-old at that time, and assuming Samudragupta to have been born in 329 BCE, he would be 51-years-old when he ascended the throne. This would be too late for a conqueror like Samudragupta, who claims in the Allahabad pillar inscription that his father gave him the throne saying that he was worthy while his eyes were filled with the tears of joy. Obviously, Chandragupta-I did not wait for old age to coronate Samudragupta. There is no record of Chandragupta-I ruling for 31 years. The first record of the Imperial Gupta regnal years is provided by Chandragupta-II, who said that it was his fifth year of reign when the Imperial Gupta year was 61. Thus it is possible that Chandragupta-I ruled for about 15 years and then placed Samudragupta on throne in 294 BCE. Thus, Chandragupta-I was about 56 years old when he abdicated the throne and Samudragupta was about 35-years-old when he ascended the throne. Rest of the revised chronology of the Imperial Guptas in Table 7.1 is derived by counting the regnal years from 309 BCE.

A revised chronology of the Vākāṭakas is shown in Table 7.2 based on the data for currently accepted chronology from "Inscriptions of the Vākāṭakas" edited by Mirashi [14]. The revised chronology is derived based on the assumption that Pravarasena-I died in 310 BCE and then calculating backward and forward using the regnal years provided by the accepted chronology.

Assuming that Samudragupta got married to the daughter of Seleucus-I Nicator in 303 BCE, it is possible that Chandragupta-II was born around 290 BCE, as he had an elder brother named Ramagupta. Samudragupta might have been busy with his military campaigns as well. This would make Chandragupta-II about 38-years-old in 252 BCE, when he ascended the throne. The marriage of his daughter Prabhāvatīguptā to the Vākāṭaka crown prince Rudrasena II could have taken place in 245 BCE, when Chandragupta-II was about 45–years-old and Prabhāvatīguptā was of a marriageable age. Kuberanāgā, mother of Prabhāvatīguptā, has been called Mahādevī in the Poona copper plate of Prabhāvatīguptā issued in the 13th year, but has been called only Devī in the Riddhapur plates of Pravarasena II issued in the 19th year [15]. This is probably related to the elevation of Dhruvadevī to the position of Mahādevī by Chandragupta-II. In the Imperial Gupta inscriptions of the successors of Chandragupta-II, Dhruvadevī has been called Mahādevī. So Kuberanāgā was already married to Chandragupta-II and became the Mahādevī when Chandragupta-II killed his brother Ramagupta and ascended the throne. Later, this position was accorded to Dhruvadevī, after Chandragupta-II married her. Chandragupta-II had to wait a while to marry Dhruvadevī to avoid public censure.

7.3 Chandragupta-II Vikramāditya

After Samudragupta, his son Chandragupta-II ascended the throne, who officially took the title of Vikramāditya. Modern historians have made Chandragupta-II as the Vikramāditya of the legends and placed Kālidāsa in his court. According to Indian tradition, Kālidāsa was in the court of Vikramāditya, who died in 57 BCE. Chandragupta-II Vikramāditya ruled in the fourth century CE according to modern historians, and third century BCE according to the chronology developed in this book. Either way, he cannot be the Vikramāditya in whose memory the Vikrama era was instituted, and whose court was adorned by Kālidāsa and rest of the nine gems. In fact, Chandragupta-II

Vikramāditya is the weakest Vikramāditya among the four historical Vikramādityas who have added to the legends of Vikramāditya. His only claim to fame in the current version of history is the defeat of Śakas for which there is no direct evidence. This has been done to prove that he was the Śakāri (enemy of the Śakas) Vikramāditya. Numismatic evidence is presented in support of this thesis, but this evidence is at best circumstantial. There are some stories about Vikramāditya that fit Chandragupta-II.

The source of the first story is the book Devīchandragupta written by Viśākhadatta. This book is not available now, but has been referenced or quoted in many later books such as the commentary on Bharata's Nāṭyaśāstra composed by Abhinavagupta, Śṛṅgāraprakāśa composed by Bhoja, Nāṭyadarpaṇa composed by Rāmachandra and Guṇachandra, and Nāṭakalaksanaratnakosa composed by Sāgaranandin [16].

According to this story, there was a king named Rāmagupta, who was hopelessly cornered by the Śakas during a war. He agreed to surrender his queen Dhruvadevī to the Śakas to secure his release. His younger brother Kumāra Chandragupta balked at this idea and instead offered to go to the enemy camp dressed as the queen and kill the Śaka king. He succeeded in his plan and saved the honour of the family. He became a hero not only for the public but the queen also, while the reputation of Rāmagupta suffered badly. Fearing for his life, Chandragupta feigned madness and killed Rāmagupta at an opportune time. Chandragupta then became the king and married Dhruvadevī.

References to this story have been made in several inscriptions by Rāṣṭrakūṭa rulers [17], which mean that this story was considered to be historical when these inscriptions were made. In the Sanjana plates, Rāṣṭrakūṭa emperor Amoghavarṣa claims superiority over a Gupta king who had killed his brother and seized the throne and the queen. In the Cambay and Sangli plates, Rāṣṭrakūṭa emperor Govinda IV claims to be as daring as Sāhasāṅka, but his reputation was not sullied by a sexual union with his brother's wife, and he did not treat his elder brother cruelly even though he could have done so if he wanted to.

This story is also found in a Muslim chronicle called Majmal-ul-Tawārīkh [18]. There was a king named Rawwāl, who had a brother named Barkamarīs. A princess had chosen Barkamarīs to be her husband, but Rawwāl got married to her. Sometime later, Rawwāl was attacked by an enemy and found refuge in a fort along with his nobles. The enemy king asked him to send his wife with a girl from each noble to get a safe passage. Rawwāl was ready to accept the proposal, but Barkamarīs proposed another plan. He dressed as the queen and killed the enemy, while the sons of other officers dressed as maids killed other officers of the enemy. A minister incited Rawwāl against Barkamarīs, who feigned madness to save himself and killed Rawwāl at an opportune time. Barkamarīs then became the king and married the widowed queen. It is obvious that in this story Rawwāl represents Rāmagupta, and Barkamarīs represents Vikramāditya. The reign of Chandragupta-II Vikramāditya was followed by his son Kumāragupta-I.

7.4 Beloved of the Gods

Kumāragupta-I ascended the throne in 213 BCE and ruled for 40 years till 173 BCE. Supposing he was about 75 years old when he died or abandoned the throne, he would have been 35-years-old when he ascended the throne. This means that he was born around 248 BCE. I have estimated earlier that Chandragupta-II was born around 290 BCE, and so he was about 42-years-old when Kumāragupta-I was born. This seems reasonable considering that Kumāragupta's mother was Dhruvadevī, who was not the first wife of Chandragupta-II. Kuberanāgā was the first wife of Chandragupta-II. Chandragupta-II married Dhruvadevī after killing his brother Ramagupta and had to wait a while to marry Dhruvadevī to avoid public criticism.

The most important event of Kumāragupta's life was his attack on Kaliṅga. As this attack took place during the eighth year of his rule, Kaliṅga was attacked in 206 BCE. Kaliṅga was so powerful and its people were such fierce warriors that even Samudragupta had not tried to subjugate them. Chandragupta-II, who had assumed the title of Vikramāditya, also thought it wise to leave Kaliṅga alone. Kumāragupta-I tried to subjugate Kaliṅga, the final frontier, but found out that the cost of this war was far beyond what he had anticipated. Kumāragupta-I managed to win the war, but the magnitude of the loss of lives in the battlefield and the sorrows of people affected by the war transformed him. In the aftermath of this war, a repentant Kumāragupta-I became a Buddhist. He assumed the title of Devānāmpriya Priyadarśī and started to spread Buddhism earnestly.

Around the same time, as Kumāragupta-I was busy planning for the Kaliṅga war or was already engaged in the war, Greek king Antiochus III Megas, who was distantly related to Kumāragupta, came to the western frontier of India. Kumāragupta's grandmother, wife of Samudragupta, was the daughter of Seleucus-I Nicator. Antiochus III Megas was the son of Seleucus II Callinicus, who was the son of Antiochus II Theos. Antiochus II Theos was the son of Antiochus-I Soter, who was the son of Seleucus-I Nicator. Thus grandmother of Kumāragupta was the sister of the great grandfather of Antiochus III Megas. Since Kumāragupta was busy with the Kaliṅga war preparation on the eastern frontier of his empire, it was Sophagasenas, possibly the viceroy of Kumāragupta, who met Antiochus III on his behalf. Antiochus III returned after receiving gifts from Sophagasenus, which included some war elephants.

The greatest contribution of Kumāragupta-I was the establishment of Nālandā University, which became a premier institute of learning. As Kumāragupta-I was the real Devānāmpriya Priyadarśī and Aśoka the Great has been granted greatness because of his erroneous identification with Devānāmpriya Priyadarśī, historians have to decide now whether Kumāragupta-I should be called Kumāragupta-I the Great.

A realistic assessment of Devānāmpriya Priyadarśī has been made by Professor Basham [19], which is that of a naïve and credulous person. In the first minor rock edict Devānāmpriya Priyadarśī claims that gods were freely mixing with men due to his strenuous faith-related activities. In the fourth rock edict he speaks of the appearance of divine chariots and balls of fire. These edicts show that Buddhists were indulging in cheap propaganda for the propagation of their faith and Kumāragupta-I was credulous enough to believe them. Here is clear proof that the use of fake miracles to convert people was started long ago by Buddhists. As it turns out others have also learnt this trick. In the 13th Rock Edict he claims that he had gained victory of Dhamma on all his frontiers as far away as the realms of Antiochus, Ptolemy, Antigonus, Magas and Alexander. However, Greek sources are totally silent about him. The effect, if at all any, was so small that it did not come to the notice of any Greek author. In the Kandahar edicts he claims that all the fishermen have stopped fishing and all the hunters have stopped hunting. This is simply impossible and no doubt he was being fed this kind of information by sycophants. This goes on to show how naïve and credulous he had become. It is a typical mindset of individuals brainwashed by religion. They lose touch with reality and start living in the make-believe world created by their own religious fantasies. While Kumāragupta-I lost touch with reality and continued to believe that his propagation of Dhamma had created a peaceful world all around, the empire was crumbling from within and barbarians were pounding at the gates. It fell upon his son Skandagupta to fight the rebellion and deter the barbarians, the acts of bravery that justified his title as Vikramāditya.

7.5 Skandagupta Vikramāditya

After Kumāragupta-I, his son Skandagupta ascended the throne and ruled for 12 years from 172-161 BCE. The next Imperial Gupta ruler after Skandagupta was

Narasiṃhagupta, but he did not include Skandagupta in the genealogy. Narasiṃhagupta lists Purugupta as his father and son of Kumāragupta. It stands to reason that Skandagupta was the step-brother of Purugupta, as Skandagupta does not name his mother in his inscriptions. We now know that Skandagupta assumed the title of Vikramāditya. We also know that Purugupta, a supposedly elder brother of Skandagupta, did not rule or ruled for a very short time. This immediately brings to mind the story of Bhartṛhari and Vikramāditya.

The story about Bhartṛhari is told in Siṃhāsana-dwātṛṃśikā (popularly known as Siṃhāsana Battīsī). There was a king called Bhartṛhari, who ruled over Ujjayinī. He had a very beautiful wife named Anaṅgasenā. King Bhartṛhari had a younger brother named Vikramāditya. A poor Brāhmaṇa received a fruit from a Goddess after propitiating her and was told by the Goddess that whoever ate that fruit would become immortal. The Brāhmaṇa gifted the fruit to king Bhartṛhari. King Bhartṛhari loved his wife dearly, so he gifted the fruit to her. The queen was in love with a servant and gave the fruit to him, who in turn gave it to a servant maid. She loved a cowherd and gave the fruit to him, who in turn gave it to a girl who carried cow dung. The girl collected the cattle droppings in a basket and put the basket on her head and placed the fruit on top of the cattle droppings. When she was walking on the road, king Bhartṛhari saw the fruit on her head. After investigation, he found the truth and was very depressed. He retired to a forest after renouncing the world. Vikramāditya became the king of Ujjayinī after Bhartṛhari renounced the throne.

This story brings us to a tantalizing prospect that Purugupta was king Bhartṛhari. We also have an interesting connection in this regard. This connection is a place called Bhitari in Uttar Pradesh, about 15 km east of the confluence of the Gomati and the Ganges rivers. Here is what Captain Wilford had to say about this place:

> Bhartrihari, according to the Hindus in general, withdrew to Chunār near Benares, where he remained some time; when his brother gave him a purganah, or small district, called to this day Bhartari, and Bhittri, after him; and which is to the eastward of the mouth of the river Gomti. There are the remains of a pretty large fort, with the ruins of his palace. [20]

So, we learn that Bhitari is a corrupt form of Bhartṛhari. We also know that Skandagupta had an inscription written on a pillar in Bhitari. This cannot be sheer coincidence. We can surmise that Bhartṛhari made his abode at Bhitari after Skandagupta provided the facility to him. As his son Narasiṃhagupta was a minor at this time, Skandagupta took over the reigns of the Imperial Gupta Empire. He had many challenges to face right from the beginning, which he has described in the Bhitari pillar inscription [21].

In line 10 of this inscription, we learn that family fortunes had fallen and Puṣyamitras had developed great power and wealth. The place of Puṣyamitras in Central India was right in the middle of the Imperial Gupta Empire. In line 12, we are told that Skandagupta recovered the ruined fortunes of his lineage by conquering his enemies by the strength of his arm. In line 14, he says again that his lineage had been made to totter and he had to establish it again. We can only imagine how bad things had become while Kumāragupta-I was sending his messengers of peace to the outside world and getting edicts on Dhamma written all over his empire. Hūṇas considered his policies as an open invitation to plunder. Luckily, they were defeated by Skandagupta as described in line 15, and India received some relief from foreign invasions for the next two decades.

There is a story about Vikramāditya in Kathāsaritsāgara [22] that fits Skandagupta as the Vikramāditya of the story. The father of Vikramāditya is called Mahendrātitya in this story. Thus the story is based on the exploits of Skandagupta Vikramāditya, whose father was Kumāragupta Mahendrātitya. The slaying of all the Mlechchhas (barbarians) by Vikramāditya is the theme of this story. The story shows that for Hindu kings, their honour and the protection of their way of life was a much higher calling than unilateral pacifism. They rejoiced at the defeat of Mlechchhas. If the barbarians dared to attack, their total defeat was the sacred duty of the Hindu kings. In Hindu scriptures, literature as well as inscriptions, the defeat of the Mlechchhas has always been described with joy and pride. Here is what Captain Wilford said about the originators of Hindu eras in 1809:

> The chronology of its kings is connected with the period of the Caliyuga; which consists of 432,000 years. This, the Hindus have divided into six unequal portions, or subordinate periods, called Śacas, because they derive their origin from six Śacas, or mighty, and glorious monarchs: three of whom have already made their appearance; and three more are expected. This system of the six Śacas, with their periods, is thus explained in the Jyotirvidābharaṇa, an astronomical treatise. Whatever

> man kills 550,000,000 Śacas (a mighty tribe of Hereticks), becomes a Śaca; and whoever kills this Śaca only, becomes a Śaca also. [23]

Now the number may be exaggerated, but the point is clear. Hindu rulers did not have the slightest compunction in going to war against invading outsiders. Hindu kings celebrated heroism, courage and valour, as did the citizens of their kingdoms.

After securing the empire from external and internal challenges, Skandagupta Vikramāditya ruled till 161 BCE at which point Narasiṃhagupta, son of Purugupta, became an adult and Skandagupta retired from active political life after handing over the reigns to Narasiṃhagupta. There was peace for over 20 years during which time the reigns of Imperial Gupta empire passed on from Narasiṃhagupta to Kumāragupta-II, and then from Kumāragupta-II to Budhagupta.

7.6 Emperor Budhagupta

The Eran Stone Pillar Inscription of Budhagupta dated Gupta era 165 (144 BCE) gives us important information to put together the final days of the Imperial Gupta empire:

> Victorious is the lord, the four-armed (god Viṣṇu) - whose couch is the broad waters of the four oceans; who is the cause of the continuance, the production, and the destruction, &c., of the universe; (and) whose ensign is Garuḍa!
> (Line 2.) - In a century of years, increased by sixty-five; and while Budhagupta (is) king; on the twelfth lunar day of the bright fortnight of the month Āshāḍha; on the day

of Suraguru; (or in figures) the year 100 (and) 60 (and) 5:-

(L. 3.) - And while Suraśmichandra is governing, with the qualities of a regent of one of the quarters of the world, (the country that lies) between the (rivers) Kālindi and Narmadā, (and) is enjoying in the world the glory of (being) a Mahārāja;-

(L. 4.) - On this (lunar day), (specified) as above by the year and month and day; — by the Mahārāja Mātriviṣṇu, who is excessively devoted to the Divine One; who, by the will of (the god) Vidhātṛ, was approached (in marriage-choice) by the goddess of sovereignty, as if by a maiden choosing (him) of her own accord (to be her husband); whose fame extends up to the borders of the four oceans; who is possessed of unimpaired honour and wealth; (and) who has been victorious in battle against many enemies;—who is the son of the son's son of Indraviṣṇu, who was attentive to his duties; who celebrated sacrifices; who practised private study (of the scriptures); who was a Brāhmaṇ saint; (and) who was the most excellent (of the followers) of the Maitrāyaṇīya (sākhā); - who is the son's son of Varuṇaviṣṇu, who imitated the virtuous qualities of (his) father; - (and) who is the son of Hariviṣṇu, who was the counterpart of (his) father in meritorious qualities, (and) was the cause of the advancement of his race;-

(L. 8.) - (By him) and by his younger brother Dhanyaviṣṇu, who is obedient to him, (and) has been accepted with favour by him, - this flag-staff of the divine (god) Janārdana, the troubler of the demons, has been erected, for the purpose of increasing the religious merit of (their) parents.

(L. 9.) - Let prosperity attend all the subjects, headed by the cows and the Brāhmaṇs! [24]

According to Śrīrāma Goyala, Budhagupta continued to rule till the Gupta era 176 or 495 CE [25]. According to the revised Imperial Gupta era of 309 BCE elaborated in this book, Budhagupta continued to rule till 133 BCE. During the time Budhagupta was ruling, the Śaka ruler Toramāṇa was building his forces to attack India.

7.7 Toramāṇa

Toramāṇa is considered a Hūṇa, though there is no evidence for it. That Toramāṇa was a Śaka, not a Hūṇa, is proven by the name of his son Mihirakula. Mihira is an ancient Persian word which also forms a part of the name of the famous astronomer Varāhamihira, a Śaka Brāhmaṇa, whose ancestors came from Persia. Though there are many literary and inscriptional references to Hūṇas in India, there is hardly any name of the leader of the Hūṇas. This point is significant not only from the point of the history of the Hūṇas, but also for the identification of emperor Vikramāditya of the Vikrama era, whose principal foreign enemy was a Śaka and not a Hūṇa. In the Eran stone boar inscription of Toramāṇa there is no mention of him being a Hūṇa [26]. This inscription was written during the first year of the rule of Toramāṇa and is from the same area where the inscription of Budhagupta was found. This inscription proves that Toramāṇa made extensive inroads inside the Imperial Gupta Empire. Eran is located in the Sagar district in Madhya Pradesh, almost in the centre of India. The inscription tells us that Toramāṇa had appointed Dhanyaviṣṇu, the younger brother of Mahārāja Mātṛviṣṇu, to rule Eran. Mahārāja Mātṛviṣṇu, who was ruling Eran under the lordship of Budhagupta, had gone to heaven. It can be concluded then that during the final days of the rule of Budhagupta, a battle was fought in Eran between the forces of Budhagupta and Toramāṇa in which Toramāṇa emerged victorious. Mahārāja Mātṛviṣṇu died fighting and Toramāṇa appointed his younger brother Dhanyaviṣṇu to rule this area. As the war was fought during the final days of the rule of Budhagupta, it took place circa 133 BCE. This date is also corroborated from an inscription of Emperor Prakāśadharmā. As the sun was setting on the Imperial Gupta Empire, a new dynasty was emerging out of its shadows to protect India from foreign invaders, and in this dynasty was born the Emperor of Indian hearts, Emperor Vikramāditya.

7.8 Rise of the Aulikaras

About 350 km west of Eran and 150 km northwest of Ujjain is the city of Mandsaur in the Malwa region in the state of Madhya Pradesh. The ancient name of this city was Daśapura. The history of Aulikaras starts here with Jayavardhana, who has been called Narendra. The name Narendra is a combination of the words Nara meaning man and Indra, King of Gods. Thus Narendra means kingly man, but we cannot be sure whether Jayavardhana was a king or his descendants have used this title to just show respect for him. Siṃhavarman was next in line and he was a king under the Lordship of the Imperial Guptas. We don't know the exact dates of the rule of Jayavardhana and Siṃhavarman, but judging from the date of Naravarman (Mālava 461 and 474), the Aulikara family started the long journey to become the paramount power of India during the reign of Samudragupta.

Table 7.3 shows the proposed timeline of Aulikara family along with the currently accepted dates. The data for Table 7.3 is taken from the genealogical chart prepared by Richard Soloman in the article, "New Inscriptional Evidence for the History of the Aulikaras of Mandasor" [27]. There were different families of Aulikaras, who gained prominence in succession. The rule of the first Aulikara family ended with Prabhākara, whose date is Mālava 524 or 178 BCE. This brings us to the second Aulikara family, in which Emperor Vikramāditya was born. The genealogy of this Aulikara family is given in the Rīsthal Inscription of Emperor Prakāśadharmā [27].

Table 7.3: The proposed timeline of the Aulikara family

Name	**Date**	**Accepted Chronology [27]**	**Proposed chronology**	**Comments**
Naravarman	Mālava 461, 474	404 CE, 417 CE	241 BCE, 228 BCE	Aulikara line 1
Viśvavarman	Kṛta 480	423 CE	222 BCE	Aulikara line 1
Bandhuvarman	Mālava 493	436 CE	209 BCE	Aulikara line 1
Prabhākara	Mālava 524	467 CE	178 BCE	Aulikara line 1
Prakāśadharmā	Mālava 572	515 CE	130 BCE	Aulikara line 2
Yaśodharmā	Mālava 589	532 CE	113 BCE	Aulikara line 2

The first person mentioned in this Aulikara line was General Dramavardhana, who has also been called Narendra. His son was king Jayavardhana. His son was king Ajitavardhana, whose son was Vibhīṣaṇavardhana. His son was Rājyavardhana, whose son was Prakāśadharmā, a crest of kings. Prakāśadharmā defeated Toramāṇa, Lord of the Hūṇas, in battle. Prakāśadharmā constructed the Vibhīṣaṇa Lake and dedicated to his grandfather Vibhīṣaṇavardhana. At the command of Prakāśadharmā, his viceroy Bhagvaddoṣa constructed the Prakāśeśvara temple, a symbol of Bhāratavarṣa (India). The inscription was made in the year 572. The eulogy was composed by Vasula, son of Kakka.

For a complete transcript of the inscription, the reader is referred to the article "New Inscriptional Evidence for the History of the Aulikaras of Mandasor" by Richard Soloman [27]. As the inscription was made in the Mālava year 572, Toramāṇa was defeated by Prakāśadharmā before the year 130 BCE. Toramāṇa was succeeded by his son Mihirakula.

7.9 Mihirakula

By all accounts, Mihirakula was a cruel emperor. Buddhist traveler Xuan Zang (Hiuen Tsiang) has accused him of persecution of the Buddhists and destruction of the monasteries. Kalhaṇa says in Rājataraṅgiṇī that Mihirakula had killed 30 million people [28]. That Mihirakula had made deep inroads inside India is evident from the following Stone Inscription of Mihirakula from Gwalior in Madhya Pradesh:

> [Om!] May he (the Sun) protect you, who is victorious,-dispelling the darkness of the banks of clouds with the masses of the multitude of his rays that light up the sky; (and) decorating the top of the side of the mountain of dawn with (his) horses, which have the tossing ends of (their) manes disheveled through the fatigue (induced) by (their) startled gait;-(and) who,-having (his) chariot-wheels (?) swallowed (?) .... the mountain of dawn; dispelling distress; (being) the light of the house which is the world; (and) effecting the destruction of night,-creates the fresh beauty of the water-lilies by (his) rays which are of the colour of molten gold.
>
> (Line 2.) – (There was) a ruler of [the earth], of great merit, who was renowned by the name of the glorious Toramāṇa; by whom, through (his) heroism that was specially characterized by truthfulness, the earth was governed with justice.
>
> (L. 3.) – Of him, the fame of whose family has risen high, the son (is) he, of unequalled prowess, the lord of the earth, who is renowned under the name of Mihirakula, (and) who, (himself) unbroken, [broke the power of] Paśupati.

(L. 4.) – While [he], the king, the remover of distress, possessed of large and pellucid eyes, is governing the earth; in the augmenting reign, (and) in the fifteenth year, of (him) the best of kings; the month Kārttika, cool and fragrant with the perfume of the red and blue waterlilies that are caused to blossom by the smiles of the rays of the moon, having come; while the spotless moon is shining; and a very auspicious day, - heralded by the chiefs of the classes of the twice-born with the noise of the proclamation of a holy day, (and) possessed of the (proper) tithi and nakshatra and muhūrta,-having arrived;-

(L. 5.) – The son's son of Matritula, and the son of Mātridāsa, by the name Mātricheṭa, an inhabitant of … on the hill, has caused to be made, on the delightful mountain which is speckled with various metals and has the appellation of Gopa, a stone-temple, the chief among the best of temples, of the Sun, for the purpose of increasing the religious merit of (his) parents and of himself, and of those who, by the … of the king, dwell on this best of mountains.

(L. 7.) – Those who cause to be made an excellent house of the Sun, like in lustre to the rays of the moon,-their abode is in heaven, until the destruction of all things!

(L. 7.) – (This) very famous proclamation of the true religion has been composed through devotion to the Sun, by him who is renowned by the name of Keśava and by… ditya.

(L. 8.) – As long as the moon shines on the thicket that is the knot of the braided hair of (the god) Śarva; and as long as the mountain Meru continues to have (its) slopes adorned by the feet of the nymphs of heaven; and as long as (the god) Viṣṇu bears the radiant (goddess) Śrī upon (his) breast which is like a dark-blue cloud;-so long

> (this) chief of [stone]-temples shall stand upon the delightful summit of the hill! [29]

This inscription was written in the 15th year of the rule of Mihirakula. We have seen that his father Toramāṇa was defeated by Prakāśadharmā shortly before 130 BCE. If Mihirakula took over the reign shortly after the defeat of Toramāṇa in 130 BCE, then this inscription was written shortly before 115 BCE. Sometime after this date Mihirakula was defeated by Emperor Yaśodharmā. It is the defeat of the Śaka king Mihirakula by Yaśodharmā that gave him the title Śakāri (Enemy of the Śakas) Vikramāditya.

7.10 Yaśodharmā the Great

There are two inscriptions that give us information about Emperor Yaśodharmā Viṣṇuvardhana. The Mandasor stone inscription of Yaśodharmā was recovered from a well in Mandsaur [30]. This inscription was written in Mālava year 589, which is 113 BCE, according to the Mālava/Kṛta era starting in 702 BCE. It tells us that the full name of the emperor was Yaśodharmā Viṣṇuvardhana and he belonged to the Aulikara clan. He had brought into subjection, with peaceful overtures and by war, the very mighty kings of the east and many (kings) of the north. With these victories he had justifiably taken the title of "supreme king of kings and supreme lord". His army had crossed the Vindhya Mountain and hence he had won territories in South India as well by 113 BCE. The important question is whether he had defeated Mihirakula by this time. We have seen above that Gwalior in Madhya Pradesh was under the control of Mihirakula. This is proven beyond doubt by inscriptional as well as numismatic evidence. Gwalior is little over 500 km north east of Mandsaur. As this inscription claims that by 113 BCE

Yaśodharmā had conquered the mighty kings of the east and many kings of the north, it is most likely that he had already defeated Mihirakula by this time.

The second inscription of Yaśodharmā called "Mandasor Pillar Inscription of Yaśodharmā" gives evidence of his victory over Mihirakula but is not dated [31]. This inscription gives more details of the exploits of Emperor Yaśodharmā Viṣṇuvardhana. He ruled over territories that were not part of the mighty Gupta Empire. He had subdued the chiefs of the Hūṇas. He had conquered the territories up to the river Lauhitya and the mountain Mahendra. Lauhitya is another name for the Brahmaputra River, which starts from Tibet and flows through Arunachal Pradesh, Assam and Bangladesh. There are two mountains that can be identified with Mahendra, one in Orissa and another in Tamil Nadu. Since the eastern boundary of Yaśodharmā's empire is already given as the Brahmaputra River, there is no need for another landmark in the east. The Mahendra then needs to be identified with the mountain of the same name in the Tirunelveli district in Tamil Nadu. This is close to the southern tip of India. He further states that his empire extended up to the Himālaya and in the west up to the ocean.

We can see that this inscription gives the boundaries of his empire in all four directions. This is again confirmed by referring to all the divisions of the earth. We now get the feel for the pan-Indian empire of Yaśodharmā Viṣṇuvardhana and realize that he was not exaggerating when he claimed that he ruled over the territories not even enjoyed by the Imperial Guptas. Here is an emperor who not only united all of India under one rule, but went beyond India's borders all the way to Bactria, as we will see shortly. No wonder people celebrated his achievements and made him the hero of the most endearing legends of ancient India.

The crowning glory of his achievement was the defeat of Mihirakula, who was a Śaka, as his name suggests. History books tell us that Mihirakula and his father Toramāṇa were Hūṇas. The claim is based on the evidence of this inscription under discussion. But there is nothing in this inscription that tells us that Mihirakula was a Hūṇa. Hūṇas are referred to in Line 4, while Mihirakula is referred to in Line 6, and in between there is Line 5 that describes the boundaries of Yaśodharmā's empire in the four directions. There is nothing in Line 5 that connects Line 4 and Line 6. The inscription clearly makes no connection between the chief of the Hūṇas and Mihirakula. Even if Mihirakula is referred as the king of the Hūṇas, it does not make Mihirakula a Hūṇa automatically. The king of the Hūṇas must not necessarily be a Hūṇa himself, just like king of the Indians during British rule was not an Indian. The following comments are truly revealing in this regard:

> In the Mandasor inscription of Yaśodharman reference is made both to Mihirakula and to the Hūṇas, but in a manner which far from connecting the two, might even suggest a definite distinction between them. … This belief rests solely upon the identification of Toramāṇa and Mihirakula (also called Mihiragula) as Hūṇa leaders. Although this view is generally assumed, there is no definitive evidence in support of it, and we cannot altogether rule out the possibility that Toramāṇa was a Kuṣāṇa chief, and being allied to the Hūṇas, was mistaken as such in India, specially because he led the Hūṇa hordes. [32]

There is a detailed story about Mihirakula in the writing of Xuan Zang (Hiuen Tsiang) [33]. Hiuen Tsiang says that the time of Mihirakula was some centuries before his arrival in India, but he came to India just after a century from Mihirakula's time, according to modern history. Clearly, his testimony favours the chronology developed in this book.

We have another piece of evidence that has a bearing on the turn of events under consideration. This evidence is the "Eran Posthumous Stone Pillar Inscription of Goparāja," and is quoted below:

> Om! In a century of years, increased by ninety-one; on the seventh lunar day of the dark fortnight of (the month) Srāvana; (or in figures) the year 100 (and) 90 (and) 1; (the month) Srāvana; the dark fortnight; the day 7:
> (Line 2.) - (There was) a king, renowned under the name of . . . rāja, sprung from the . . . laksha (?) lineage; and his son (was) that very valorous king (who was known) by the name (of) Mādhava.
> (L. 3.) - His son was the illustrious Goparāja, renowned for manliness; the daughter's son of the Sarabha king; who is (even) now (?) the ornament of (his) lineage.
> (L. 5.) - (There is) the glorious Bhānugupta, the bravest man on the earth, a mighty king, equal to Pārtha, exceedingly heroic; and, along with him, Goparāja followed . . . (his) friends (and came) here. [And] having fought a very famous battle, he, [who was but little short of being equal to] the celestial [king (Indra)], (died and) went to heaven; and (his) devoted, attached, beloved, and beauteous wife, in close companionship, accompanied (him) onto the funeral pyre. [34]

The ruling monarch on the side of Goparāja is mentioned as Bhānugupta, and the year is mentioned as 191. Since the ruling monarch is a Gupta, it can be assumed that the era under consideration is the Gupta era. According to the Imperial Gupta era starting in 309 BCE, year 191 of this era will fall in 118 BCE. The question is, who was the adversary that Bhānugupta and Goparāja were fighting? Based on the discussion in this chapter, we already know that Toramāṇa was defeated by Prakāśadharmā before 130 BCE, and Mihirakula was defeated by Yaśodharmā before 113 BCE. In between 130 BCE and 113

BCE, Mihirakula ruled for 15 years. It seems that the likely sequence of events is as follows: shortly before 130 BCE Imperial Guptas were attacked by Toramāṇa. The Gupta ruler fled and hid somewhere. While Toramāṇa was returning, he was attacked by Prakāśadharmā, who was a subordinate of the Gupta ruler. Toramāṇa lost the battle and Prakāśadharmā declared independence from the Gupta ruler. After Toramāṇa's defeat at the hands of Prakāśadharmā, Toramāṇa's son Mihirakula took over the empire. Yaśodharmā was probably less than ten-years-old at this time as he died in 57 BCE, some 73 years later. Mihirakula took time to build his military strength and attacked the Imperial Gupta ruler Bhānugupta in 118 BCE. Bhānugupta was defeated and Goparāja lost his life in the battle. It fell on the Aulikaras then to defend India from the cruel Śaka ruler Mihirakula. By this time Yaśodharmā was in his twenties and raring to defend India from the Śakas and other foreign rulers. Sometime before 113 BCE, a decisive battle was fought between Yaśodharmā and Mihirakula in which Mihirakula's forces were totally uprooted. Mihirakula had to put his head on Yaśodharmā's feet and beg for mercy.

After making sure that Mihirakula posed no danger to him, Yaśodharmā embarked on a mission to unify India under one rule. Though his inscriptions don't give the exact route of his conquests, we can get this information from the epic Raghuvaṃśa poem written by Kālidāsa. Kālidāsa was one of the nine jewels in the court of Emperor Yaśodharmā Viṣṇuvardhana Vikramāditya. Another famous personality among the nine jewels was the astronomer Varāhamihira. We have seen that Yaśodharmā was from Mandsaur, and Mandsaur was known as Daśapura in ancient times. It cannot be a coincidence that this small town called Daśapura is mentioned by Varāhamihira in Bṛhatsaṃhitā [35] and by Kālidāsa in Meghadūta [36]. Obviously, they had their patron Yaśodharmā Viṣṇuvardhana in mind while writing these texts.

Śrīrāma Goyala is of the opinion that Kālidāsa has written the account of the conquests of Raghu based on the route followed by Samudragupta [37]. However, this opinion is based on the faulty chronology. As Kālidāsa was a junior contemporary of Yaśodharmā, he did not have to look elsewhere for inspiration. According to the description of Raghu's conquests in Raghuvaṃśa [38], the route taken by Raghu was as follows [39-40]. He started by going eastward and conquering Suhma (West Bengal) and Vaṅga (South Bengal delta region). Utkala (North-eastern Odisha) was next followed by Kaliṅga (Southern Odisha, Eastern Telangana and Northern Andhra Pradesh). He continued south and crossed the Kaveri River. He then followed the eastern coast to the southern tip of India. On the way to the Malay mountain, the Pāṇḍya king paid his obeisance. He then turned northward to continue along the west coast. He crossed the Sahya Mountain and conquered the kingdoms on the west coast including Kerala. After continuing further, he turned west and conquered the Persians. Then Raghu turned north and went to the banks of Oxus and subdued the Hūṇas and Kambojas. He turned eastward again and conquered the kingdoms along the Himalayas, which included the Kirātas (inhabitants of Nepal) and Utsavasaṅketas (a tribe of the mountains who passed their lives in feasting and conviviality [41]). He then crossed the Lauhitya River and subdued the king of Prāgjyotiṣa/ Kāmarūpa (present day Assam). This is where the Digvijaya (global conquest) of Raghu was completed.

We have many similarities between this description and the conquests made by Yaśodharmā. Yaśodharmā has mentioned his conquests up to the Lauhitya River, which is also part of Raghu's conquests. Raghu conquered the Hūṇas, so did Yaśodharmā. Raghu conquered the regions along the Himalayas, so did Yaśodharmā. As Yaśodharmā mentions the Mahendra Mountain on the southern tip of India under his empire, he could have followed the same route that Raghu is supposed to have taken.

Raghu's horses are supposed to have relieved their fatigue by rolling on the banks of the river Oxus. River Oxus is the Amu Darya in Central Asia, which was known as Vaṅkṣu in ancient India. On its banks was the kingdom of Bactria, modern day Balkh at the northern border of Afghanistan, close to Uzbekistan. In ancient India this area was known as Vāhlika and was often juxtaposed with Kambojas. We will now present evidence that Yaśodharmā had made conquests up to Vāhlika. The evidence comes from an inscription on the famous Delhi Iron pillar, which is located in the Qutb complex in Mehrauli.

Mehrauli is deformation of the original name of this locality, which was Mihirāwalī. It was named after the famous astronomer Varāhamihira. An astronomical complex was made here in honour of Varāhamihira, which consisted of twenty seven buildings, one for each nakṣatra (asterism). An iron pillar honouring the patron of Varāhamihira, Emperor Vikramāditya, was brought from Viṣṇupadagiri, and erected in this complex. In honour of Emperor Yaśodharmā Viṣṇuvardhana, the real Vikramāditya behind the legends, the pillar was named Viṣṇudhvaja as referred to in the last line of the Iron Pillar inscription. This astronomical complex was destroyed by invaders after the defeat of Prithvīrāj Chauhān towards the end of twelfth century CE, and a mosque called Quwwat-ul-Islam (Might of Islam) took its place. A still extant plaque outside the mosque, which was written by invaders soon after the destruction of the astronomical complex, proclaims that the mosque was made by destroying twenty seven temples. Number 27 is the key here, as this is the number of nakṣatras according to Hindu astronomy. As Hindus had adorned the astronomical complex with exquisite sculptures, this astronomical complex was mistaken as temples by the invaders. The inscription on the Mehrauli iron pillar has immortalized the fame of Vikramāditya Yaśodharmā Viṣṇuvardhana. It is quoted below for further discussion:

He, on whose arm fame was inscribed by the sword, when, in battle in the Vanga countries, he kneaded (and turned) back with (his) breast the enemies who, uniting together, came against (him); he, by whom, having crossed in warfare the seven mouths of the (river) Sindhu, the Vāhlikas were conquered; - he, by the breezes of whose prowess the southern ocean is even still perfumed;

(Line 3.) - He, the remnant of the great zeal of whose energy, which utterly destroyed (his) enemies, like (the remnant of the great glowing heat) of a burned-out fire in a great forest, even now leaves not the earth; though he, the king, as if wearied, has quitted this earth, and has gone to the other world, moving in (bodily) form to the land (of paradise) won by (the merit of has) actions, (but) remaining on (this) earth by (the memory of his) fame;

(L. 5.) - By him, the king, - who attained sole supreme sovereignty in the world, acquired by his own arm and (enjoyed) for a very long time; (and) who, having the name of Chandra, carried a beauty of countenance like (the beauty of) the full-moon, having in faith fixed his mind upon (the god) Viṣṇu, this lofty standard of the divine Viṣṇu was set up on the hill (called) Viṣṇupada. [42]

The use of word Viṣṇu three times in the last sentence reinforces the conclusion that this iron pillar commemorates the victories of Vikramāditya Yaśodharmā Viṣṇuvardhana. Historians have various theories about the identity of the king mentioned in this inscription. Most of them have focused on kings having the name Chandra, such as Chandragupta Maurya, Chandrāṃśa, Sadāchandra, Chandravarmā, Chandragupta-I, and Chandragupta-II [43]. Śrīrāma Goyala has identified this king with Samudragupta, as he considers him to be the only king who had made extensive conquests justifying this identification [44]. However, Vikramāditya Yaśodharmā Viṣṇuvardhana fulfills this criterion better. The only objection to this identification is the name Chandra for the king in this inscription. Chandra (moon) in this inscription refers to the name of the dynasty of Yaśodharmā Viṣṇuvardhana, which was Aulikara. Here is the opinion of noted historian D. C. Sircar regarding the meaning of Aulikara:

> The real meaning of auli is uncertain; sometimes aulikara is interpreted as himakara or the moon. [45]

Vikramāditya Yaśodharmā was not only a great warrior, but also a great patron of learning. His court was adorned with very talented people from all fields of knowledge. Nine of them were most notable and were called the nine gems of his court. An astrological text, Jyotirvidābharaṇa, gives the name of the nine gems in the court of Vikramāditya. Jyotirvidābharaṇa is supposedly written by Kālidāsa, but modern historians consider this text to be a forgery. Bhāo Dājī has given the following information about Vikramāditya from the text Jyotirvidābharaṇa:

> The conclusion to the Jyotirvidābharaṇa, which contains the verse respecting the "nine gems" so frequently quoted as a "memorial verse" without any one having been able to trace it to source, is given entire below, as the author enters into chronological details regarding himself not met with in any of the well known works of the great Kālidāsa.
>
> Translation of Chapter 22, containing twenty-one verses.
>
> 1. I now proceed to give in order the subjects already treated of, and to describe the joy producing monarch, Vikrama.
>
> [The 2nd to the 6th verse contains the names of the subjects, and the 6th verse states that the total number of

verses in the book are 1,424, and that the book is named "Jyotirvidābharaṇa Kāyva."]

7. By me has this work been produced in the reign of Vikrama over Mālava in Bhārata Varsha, which is rendered delightful by the study of the Śrutis and Smṛtis, and which contains 180 countries.

8. Śaṅku, Vararuchi, Maṇi, Anśudatta, Jishṇu, Trilochana, Hari, Ghaṭakharpara, also Amara Sinha and other poets, adorned his assembly.

9. Satya, Varāha Mihira, Śrita Sena, Śrī Bādarāyaṇa, Maṇittha, and Kumāra Sinha, were the astronomers, and myself and other professors of astronomy also.

10. Dhanwantari, Kṣapaṇaka, Amarasinha, Śaṅku, Vetālabhaṭṭa, Ghaṭakharpara, Kālidāsa, the renowned Varāha Mihira and Vararuchi, are the nine gems of Vikrama.

11. Vikrama flourished, and at his court attended 800 Mandalika (minor) Rajas; and at the great assembly there were 16 eloquent pundits, 10 astronomers, 6 physicians, and 16 reciters of the Vedas.

12. His army occupied 18 yojanas of ground; his forces consisted of 3 crores of infantry, 10 crores of cavalry, 24,300 elephants, and 400,000 boats. No monarch could be compared to him.

13. He celebrated his victory over the world by the destruction of ninety-five Śaka chiefs, and established his era in the Kaliyuga; and by daily giving in alms, pearls, gold, jewels, cows, horses and elephants, he brightened the face of Dharma.

14. He destroyed the proud king of Dravida, also the king of Lāṭa, defeated the king of Gauda, and conquered

him of Gurjaradeśa, removed the darkness of Dhārā, delighted the king of Kamboja, and conducted himself with success.

15. His prowess and qualities were like those of Indra, Ambhodhī, Amaradru, Smara and Meru. He was the delight of his subjects, and humbled his enemies by conquering and restoring their forts to them.

16. He protects the capital Ujjayinī, the great city which gives beatitude to its inhabitants, and which is celebrated for the presence of Mahākāla.

17. In a great battle he conquered the king of the Śakas in Ruma, paraded his royal prisoner in Ujjayinī, and afterwards set him free. Such was his irresistible prowess.

18. Whilst Vikrama thus reigned in Avanti, the people enjoyed prosperity, happiness, and wealth, and the injunctions of the Vedas were everywhere observed.

19. Śaṅku and many other pundits and poets, and Varāha Mihira and other astronomers, flourished at his court. They respect the genius of me, who am a friend of the king.

20. Having first composed three Kāvyas, i.e. the Raghuvanśa and others, I composed several treatises on Vedic subjects (Śriti Karmavāda); then from Kālidāsa proceeded the astrological treatise called Jyotirvidābharaṇa.

21. 3068 years of Kali having passed, in the month of Vyśākha I commenced composing the work, and completed it in the month of Kārtika. Having zealously examined many astronomical works, I have composed this treatise for the edification of astronomers. [46]

Though the authenticity of Jyotirvidābharaṇa has been questioned, it should be kept in mind that even according to colonial historians this text was written long before British came to India. The information contained in these verses was believed to be true when Jyotirvidābharaṇa was written. These verses provide us with a wealth of information about the most endearing monarch of ancient India.

A major point is the specification of the place where the epic battle was fought between Vikrāmāditya Yaśodharmā and the Śaka ruler Mihirakula. This battle was fought in Rumā, which is near Sambhar Lake between Ajmer and Jaipur in Rajasthan. This place is about 400 km north of Mandsaur, and fits the description of the area where the battle could have been fought, if we keep in mind that Mihirakula entered India through the plains of Punjab and had extended his rule up to Gwalior in Madhya Pradesh, which is about 400 km east of Rumā. As Yaśodharmā's family was ruling from Mandsaur to begin with, and Mihirakula had taken over most of the area north of Yaśodharmā's kingdom, a battle between them in Rumā implies that Yaśodharmā had initiated the battle by taking his forces up north in Mihirakula's territory. We should keep in mind that Mihirakula was a barbarian foreigner (mlechchha) and getting rid of mlechchhas was an honourable duty of Indian kings. After the battle, Mihirakula was held captive and paraded in Ujjayinī before being set free. This is consistent with Yaśodharmā's inscription in which it is said that Mihirakula had to bow his head at Yaśodharmā's feet, but nothing is said about executing him.

We next come to the nine gems in Vikrāmāditya's court. Verse 10 of Chapter 22 of Jyotirvidābharaṇa gives the names of nine gems in the court of emperor Vikrāmāditya -- Dhanwantari, Kṣapaṇaka, Amarasiṃha, Śaṅku, Vetālabhaṭṭa, Ghaṭakarpara, Kālidāsa, Varāhamihira and Vararuchi. These nine celebrities were the most noted in the court of Vikrāmāditya among many more luminaries such as Maṇi, Anśudatta, Jiṣṇu, Trilochana, Hari, Satya, Śrita Sena, Śrī Bādarāyaṇa, Maṇittha, and Kumāra Sinha.

The tradition of nine gems or Navaratna is engrained in the collective memory of the Hindus. Even Akbar tried to duplicate it after he came to know of it. Before him, king Bhoja is also supposed to have had nine gems in his court. There exists a short text called Navaratna, which was written to preserve this tradition. Goonetilleke has provided us information about this text and the prevailing wisdom of the time in the nineteenth century in his paper [47]. There are many points to note from this paper. First, we have conclusive evidence that the tradition of nine gems in the court of Vikramāditya is a very well-established tradition. It was considered so sacrosanct that it was memorized from generation to generation using mnemonics. Second, the evidence of Jyotirvidābharaṇa is so damning to the accepted chronology that colonial historians went hammer and tongs at it to discredit it. Whether it was written in 33 BCE by Kālidāsa or someone else claiming to be Kālidāsa several centuries later, since it was written before the arrival of Europeans in India, the traditions described in it genuinely represent what was believed by Indians for centuries.

There indeed was an emperor Vikramāditya in the first century BCE, whose empire not only included most of current day India, Bangladesh and Pakistan, but extended up to Bactria of yesteryears. There should be no reason now to doubt the authenticity of the tradition of nine gems of emperor Vikramāditya. There is also inscriptional evidence for Amarasiṃha being in the court of emperor Vikramāditya during the first century BCE as follows:

> An inscription found by Mr. Wilkins at Buddha Gayā, of which he published a translation in Asiatic Researches (I, 284), and which was written to commemorate the foundation of a temple of Buddha by Amara Siṃha, bears the date 1005 of the era of Vikramāditya, answering to the Christian year 949: the authenticity of this inscription we have no reason to question, as it professes no object to which suspicion of fraud or interest can be attached, and it is perfectly consistent with the character and traditions of the place in which it was found: the identity of the person is also indisputable, as all ancient authorities concur in representing Amara as a worshipper of Buddha, and he is designated in the inscription in the usual manner as one of the nine gems of Vikramāditya's court. ... The author states that his having derived his knowledge of Amara's being the founder of the temple from its records, or as it is translated "from the authority of the place", an authority which no doubt existed, as most celebrated shrines are furnished with a legend, a lying one it may be granted, which professes to give their history: and it matters not here, of what description was the record of the temple of Buddhas, as, if in the middle of the tenth century it had converted Amara Sinha into the hero of a holy fable, it at least proves his prior and remote existence.

> To return to the inscription: the writer states that "Amara was the favourite and minister of Vikramāditya, who was certainly a king renowned in the world", and whom he intends by Vikramāditya can scarcely be doubted, as he dates from that prince's era: it is therefore perfectly clear that at so distant a period as A.D. 949, if the inscription is to be trusted, the same traditional account of Amara's date prevailed, which is still received, and however accurate or incorrect this tradition may have been, its existence is fatal to the supposition that the subject of it was alive at the period when such a belief was current, and still more so to the opinion we have noticed of his flourishing at some subsequent date.
>
> That the inscription is worthy of credit, I see no reason to doubt, and it is assuredly an authority of more weight than the notions of nameless Paṇḍits, the sole impugners of the belief it sanctions. [48]

Let us see if there is anything known about the remaining four gems -- Kṣapaṇaka, Śaṅku, Vetālabhaṭṭa, and Ghaṭakharpara. Monier-Williams' Sanskrit-English dictionary gives information about three of them -- Kṣapaṇaka, Vetālabhaṭṭa, and Ghaṭakharpara. Kṣapaṇaka means a religious mendicant, typically a Jain mendicant, who wears no garments, and was perhaps the Jain astronomer Siddhasena [49]. Vetālabhaṭṭa was a poet and author of Nīti-pradīpa [50]. Ghaṭakharpara was a poet, who wrote a poem named after him, and was also the author of Nīti-sāra [51]. Śaṅku is considered to be an architect [52] or a poet and educationist [53].

We now have a picture of an emperor par excellence, whose court was filled with learned people from all walks of life. He was a great patron of learning and his generosity was legendary. As India suffered under the attacks of the barbarians one after another, the fascination with emperor Vikramāditya grew. It became the stuff of legends – of an emperor who had chased the barbarians all the way to Bactria. Over time, he became the hero of a number of fables, as described in the Vetālapañchaviṃśati (popularly known as Vetāla Pachīsī), Siṃhāsana-dwātṛṃśikā (popularly known as Siṃhāsana Battīsī), and Śuka-saptaśatī (popularly known as the story of a Parrot and a Mynah). In the popular imagination, Vikramāditya was a paragon of virtue, a just ruler, a generous king, and a warrior par excellence.

As described in the Delhi Iron Pillar inscription, Vikramāditya Yaśodharmā enjoyed life for a long time, and when he passed away in 57 BCE at an advanced age, an era came to an end. The people of India instituted the Vikrama era to preserve his memory. It is the testimony of their love that the Vikrama era continues to be in use even today. Even though Emperor Vikramāditya Yaśodharmā left this world more than 2000 years ago, Indians continue to cherish his memory.

Notes

1. Fleet (1888): 241.
2. Pargiter (1913): 72-73.
3. Mookerji (1973): 19.
4. Mirashi (1974): 33.
5. Bakshi and Ralhan (2007): 103.
6. McCrindle (1893): 327-328.
7. McCrindle (1893): 310-311.
8. McCrindle (1893): 310.
9. McCrindle (1901): 88-89.

10. Fleet (1888): 20-21.
11. Fleet (1888): 10-17.
12. Goyal (1987b): 67.
13. Willis (2005).
14. Mirashi (1963): vi.
15. Jain (1972): 232.
16. Sircar (1969): 138.
17. Sircar (1969): 141.
18. Sircar (1969): 143-145.
19. Basham (1982).
20. Wilford (1809b). Quote on pages 152-153.
21. Fleet (1888): 54-56.
22. Penzer (1928): 2-6.
23. Wilford (1809a). Quote on page 82.
24. Fleet (1888): 90.
25. Goyala (1987a): 338.
26. Fleet (1888): 160-161.
27. Saloman (1989).
28. Rājataraṅgiṇī 1.310.
29. Fleet (1888): 163-164.
30. Fleet (1888): 154-158.
31. Fleet (1888): 147-148.
32. Majumdar and Altekar (1967): 197-198.
33. Beal (1884):165-172.
34. Fleet (1888): 93.
35. Bṛhatsaṃhitā XIV.2.
36. Meghadūta 1.49. (Daśapura Vadhūnetra kautūhalānām).
37. Goyala (1987b): 264-265.
38. Raghuvaṃśa 4.32-84.
39. Goyala (1987b): 264-265.
40. Gopal (1984): 59-60.
41. Duncker (1880): 428.
42. Fleet (1888): 141-142.
43. Goyala (1987b): 48-49.

44. Goyala (1987b): 50-56.
45. Sircar (1966): 37.
46. Dājī (1861).
47. Goonetilleke (1884).
48. Rost (1865): 180-182.
49. Monier-Williams (1988): 326.
50. Monier-Williams (1988): 1015.
51. Monier-Williams (1988): 375.
52. Chatterjee (1998): 223.
53. Nirmala (1992): 131.

"The most dangerous untruths are truths slightly distorted."

- Georg Christoph Lichtenberg

8. India after Vikramāditya

When Vikramāditya Yaśodharmā Viṣṇuvardhana passed away in 57 BCE, the empire he had built quickly disintegrated. This provided a golden opportunity for invaders to seize a piece of the empire. While modern historians have made most Indians the descendants of invaders, the native tradition has been quite the opposite. There is no denying that foreigners came to India throughout history, but they came in small numbers and were simply assimilated by the native population. The Indian population was always far greater than the outsiders/invaders. Neither the so-called Aryans nor the Rajputs came to India from outside. According to native Indian traditions, Indians were always in India. This is in perfect agreement with the population density of India, which has always been high due to its temperate climate. The history of India has been written by foreigners, and they have glorified their own accomplishments and hidden or marginalized India's victories and civilizational strengths. To discover the Indian version of events, we need to carefully analyze the native Indian sources as well as the account of the foreigners. The clues to fixing the chronology of India, during the first millennium, lie in Persia, the land of the Śakas.

8.1 The Land of the Śakas

According to modern historians, the Śakas were Scythians from Central Asia. According to Manusmṛti, the Śakas were originally Kshatriyas, who lost their status due to their omission of holy rites [1]. Among the many tribes outside India such as the Kambojas, Yavanas, Śakas, Pahlavas, Chinas, and Kiratas, it was the Śakas who captured a large part of Western India after the death of Vikramāditya Yaśodharmā Viṣṇuvardhana. The Śakas came from the historical Sistan region, which was named Śakasthāna earlier. Śakasthāna means the land of the Śakas. Sistan or Śakasthāna was spread around the meeting point of Iran, Pakistan and Afghanistan. Śakasthāna was spread over parts of current day Sistan and Balochistan province in Iran, Nimruz in Afghanistan, and Balochistan in Pakistan. The migration of Śakas towards India started with the invasion of their land by Alexander, the ancestors of Varāhamihira being one of them. Later, the tyrannical Śaka ruler Mihirakula was defeated by Vikramāditya Yaśodharmā Viṣṇuvardhana. After the death of emperor Yaśodharmā, his empire disintegrated. This gave the Śakas the opportunity to consolidate power in Western India. As the Śakas grew stronger and started to expand their empire, they were challenged by a mighty emperor with his seat of power at Pratiṣṭhāna, current day Paithan in Aurangabad district in Maharashtra.

8.2 The Śālivāhana Śaka Era

The defeat of the Śakas at the hands of the Sātavāhana emperor Gautamīputra Śātakarṇi in 78 CE is a celebrated event in the native history of India. The Śālivāhana Śaka was instituted to commemorate the uprooting of the Śaka kings by Śālivāhana Gautamīputra Śātakarṇi. Modern historians have given credit to foreign rulers such as the Kuṣāṇa emperor Kaniṣka or the Śaka ruler Chaṣṭana for instituting this era. As in the case of the Vikrama era, they have ignored native traditions. They refuse to acknowledge that "Śaka" in Śālivāhana Śaka means an era and not a foreigner. Doing so will open a can of worms. How did the word "Śaka" originally meaning a certain foreign tribe come to mean an era? When a word acquires additional meaning there is usually a reason for it. In this case it was the use of "Śaka" era by Varāhamihira who started the use of Cyrus Śaka era in India in second century BCE. The Cyrus Śaka era named after Cyrus the Great of Persia had a zero point of 550 BCE, corresponding to the foundation of the Achaemenid Empire. Gradually, the word Śaka became equivalent to an era. It is quite obvious by the use of the word "Śakakāraka", which means creator of the Śaka. During the colonial era, every Hindu calendar had the list of six Śakakārakas or creators of the era, three of them past, and three of them still to come. Let us look at the evidence presented in a paper in 1875 by Rāo Sāheb Vishvanāth Nārāyaṇ Maṇḍalik:

> Śālivāhana, sometimes called Śātavāhana or Sātavāhana, is the name of the Hindu king after whom the present Śaka era current in Mahārāshṭra is named. … When a Marāṭhā Hindu makes a religious determination about

anything, he has to repeat the period of time that has elapsed since the advent of the Kali-yuga, the number of the incarnation believed to preside over the destinies of the world, the geographical position occupied by the performer of the ceremony, and the time with reference to the Śālivāhana era in the calendar. This is the era generally observed to the south of the Narmadā. To the north of that river, the Vikramāditya era is observed in most places.

In the popular enumeration of the founders of Śakās or eras, Śālivāhana stands the third. Thus,

> Yudhishṭhiro Vikrama Śālivāhanau,
> Tato Nṛpaḥ Syādvijayābhinandanaḥ;
> Tatastu Nāgārjunabhūpatiḥ Kalau,
> Kalkī shaḍete Śakakārakāḥ Smṛtāḥ.

Translation:— In the Kali age (come) Yudhishṭhira, Vikrama, (and) Śālivāhana, afterwards will be the king Vijayābhinandana, then the king Nāgārjuna, (and) the sixth Kalki: these six are stated to be the makers of śakās or eras.

The calculators of the current native almanacs describe the places of these founders, and the duration of their eras. Thus, beginning with the first, Yudhishṭhira, he is stated to have lived at Indraprastha (supposed to be somewhere near Dehli), and the duration of his era to be 3044 years, up to the time of Vikrama of Ujjayinī, whose era is said to have extended to 135 years, until the advent of Śālivāhana at Pratishṭhāna, whose era will, it is said, last 18,000 years. He will be succeeded by the following:—

(4.) The fourth, Vijayābhinandana, at Vaitaraṇī, at the junction of the Indus; his era 10,000 years.

> (5.) The fifth, Nāgārjuna, at Dhārātīrtha, in the Gauḍa country; his era 400,000 years.
>
> (6.) The sixth, Kalkin, at Karavīra-pattana [or Kolhāpura], in the Karnāṭaka; his era 821 years.
>
> The Śaka year of Śālivāhana begins on the first day of the first half of Chaitra. [2]

The verse quoted above listing the six creators of eras has also been reproduced in a paper written by Pandit Jwālā Sahāya in 1893 [3]. Thus, there should not be any problem in crediting the Śālivāhana Śaka era to its founder Gautamīputra Śātakarṇi. The establishment of Śālivāhana Śaka era in 78 CE by Gautamīputra Śātakarṇi gives us a chronological marker for the Sātavāhana dynasty.

8.3 The Sātavāhana and Śaka Chronology

The Sātavāhana dynasty is currently known as Āndhra-Sātavāhana dynasty. This is based on the evidence from Purāṇas that list the Sātavāhana rulers as Āndhras. However, Sātavāhana rulers have never referred to themselves as Āndhras in any of their inscriptions. The seat of power of the Sātavāhanas was on west coast of South India in present day Maharashtra, while the Āndhras ruled from the east coast. In the inscriptions of Devānāmpriya Priyadarśī or Kumāragupta-I, Āndhras have been differentiated from Satiyaputra, which possibly refers to the Sātavāhanas. Chronologically, the Āndhras became a powerful force several centuries earlier than the Sātavāhanas. Modern historians have created the Sātavāhana chronology based on the information contained in the Purāṇas as well as in the inscriptions of the Sātavāhana rulers. There is no unanimity regarding the

Sātavāhana chronology. Table 8.1 shows two different versions of the currently accepted Sātavāhana chronology.

Table 8.1: Currently accepted Sātavāhana chronology

Kings	**Modern Chronology I**	**Modern Chronology II [6]**
Simuka (Chimuka)	c. 235-212 BCE [4]	c. 52 - c. 30 BCE
Kṛṣṇa (Kanha)	c. 212-195 BCE [4]	c. 29 - c. 12 BCE
Śātakarṇi I	c. 195-193 BCE [4]	c. 12 BCE - c. 44 CE
Vediśrī and Satiśrī	c. 193-166 BCE [4]	
Śātakarṇi II	166-111 BCE [4]	
Hāla	20-24 CE [4]	
Gautamīputra Śātakarṇi	106-130 CE [5]	c. 61-90 CE
Vāsiṣṭhīputra Pulumāvi	130-159 CE [5]	c. 91-118 CE
Vāsiṣṭhīputra Śātakarṇi		c. 119-147 CE
Vāsiṣṭhīputra Śivaśrī Pulumāvi	159-166 CE [5]	c. 148-155 CE
Vāsiṣṭhīputra Skanda Śātakarṇi	167-174 CE [5]	c. 156-170 CE
Gautamīputra Yajñaśrī Śātakarṇi	174-203 CE [5]	c. 171-199 CE
Gautamīputra Vijaya Śātakarṇi	203-209 CE [5]	c. 200-205 CE
Vāsiṣṭhīputra Chanḍaśrī Śātakarṇi	209-219 CE [5]	c. 206-215 CE
Vāsiṣṭhīputra Vijaya Śātakarṇi		c. 216-225 CE
Vāsiṣṭhīputra Pulumāvi (Pulomā)	219-227 CE [5]	c. 226-232 CE

As can be seen from Table 8.1, there is a wide difference in the chronology of early Sātavāhana rulers. The Purāṇas list up to 30 Āndhra (Sātavāhana) rulers. Though the Vāyu, Brahmāṇḍa, Bhāgavata, and Viṣṇu Purāṇas say that there were 30 kings, not all of them list all the kings [7]. In addition, only some of the 30 Sātavāhana rulers are known from inscriptions. This has given the historians the leverage to choose how many rulers they consider historical. Also, modern historians have placed the Suṅga and Kaṇva rulers during the two centuries before the Common Era leading to a big gap in the middle of the Sātavāhana chronology. An alternative Sātavāhana chronology is shown in Table 8.2 below.

The proposed chronology is based on the complete list of 30 rulers of the Sātavāhana dynasty along with the length of their reign as given in the Purāṇas and placing the beginning of Śālivāhana Śaka era (78 CE) during the reign of Gautamīputra Śātakarṇi. The Śālivāhana Śaka era was instituted to celebrate the extirpation of Kṣaharata Śakas by Gautamīputra Śātakarṇi. The Kṣaharāta Śakas ruled for a short period, with prominent rulers being Bhūmaka, his son Nahapāna, and Nahapāna's son-in-law Uṣavadata (Ṛṣabhadatta). Since Gautamīputra Śātakarṇi extirpated the Kṣaharāta Śakas in the eighteenth year of his reign [9], he ascended the throne in 61 CE and reigned till 85 CE.

After the defeat of the Kṣaharāta Śakas, another branch of Śakas called the Kārdamaka Śakas came into prominence. They ruled for a long period of time. The list of Kārdamaka Śaka rulers along with their known regnal years are shown in Table 8.3. Modern historians have counted these years from the beginning of the Śālivāhana Śaka era (78 CE). Some of them believe that the first Kārdamaka Śaka ruler Chaṣṭana founded the Śālivāhana Śaka era, while others simply count from this era as there is really no other era available to refer to.

Table 8.2: The Sātavāhana chronology (Proposed)

	Name	Years ruled [8]	Reign
1	Simuka	23	c. 281-258 BCE
2	Kṛṣṇa	10	c. 258-248 BCE
3	Śrī -Śātakarṇi	10	c. 248-238 BCE
4	Pūrnotsaṅga	18	c. 238-220 BCE
5	Skandhastambhi	18	c. 220-202 BCE
6	Śātakarṇi	56	c. 202-146 BCE
7	Lambodara	18	c. 146-128 BCE
8	Āpīlaka	12	c. 128-116 BCE
9	Meghasvāti	18	c. 116-98 BCE
10	Svāti	18	c. 98-80 BCE
11	Skandasvāti	7	c. 80-73 BCE
12	Mṛgendra Svātikarṇa	3	c. 73-70 BCE
13	Kuntala Svātikarṇa	8	c. 70-62 BCE
14	Svātivarṇa	1	c. 62-61 BCE
15	Pulomāvi	36	c. 61-25 BCE
16	Ariṣṭakarṇa	25	c. 25 BCE- 1 CE
17	Hāla	5	c. 1-6 CE
18	Mantalaka	5	c. 6-11 CE
19	Purindraṣeṇa	21	c. 11-32 CE
20	Sundara Śātakarṇi	1	c.32-33 CE
21	Chakora Śātakarṇi	0.5	c.33 CE
22	Śivasvāti	28	c.33-61 CE
23	Gautamīputra	21	c.61-85 CE*
24	Pulomā	28	c.85-113 CE
25	Śivaśrī Pulomā	7	c.113-120 CE
26	Śivaskandha Śātakarṇi	3	c.120-123 CE
27	Yajñaśrī Śātakarṇika	29	c.123-152 CE
28	Vijaya	6	c.152-158 CE
29	Chanḍaśrī Śātakarṇi	10	c.158-168 CE
30	Pulomāvi	7	c. 168-175 CE

*24 years were used for the period of reign based on inscriptional evidence.

Table 8.3: Kārdamaka Śaka genealogy [10]

Kings	**Relation**	**Title**	**Years known**
Chaṣṭana	Son of Yasamotika	Mahākṣatrapa	52
Jayadāman	Son of Chaṣṭana	Did not rule	
Rudradāman	Son of Jayadāman	Mahākṣatrapa	72
Dāmajadaśrī*	Son of Rudradāman	Mahākṣatrapa	
Jīvadāman	Son of Dāmajadaśrī,	Mahākṣatrapa	100, 119-121
Rudrasiṃha I	Brother of Dāmajadaśrī	Kṣatrapa	102, 110-112
		Mahākṣatrapa	103-110, 113-118
Satyadāman	Son of Dāmajadaśrī,	Kṣatrapa	
Rudrasena I	Son of Rudrasiṃha I	Kṣatrapa	121
		Mahākṣatrapa	122-144
Saṅghadāman	Son of Rudrasiṃha I	Mahākṣatrapa	144-145
Dāmasena	Son of Rudrasiṃha I	Mahākṣatrapa	145-158
Pṛthīvisena	Son of Rudrasena I	Kṣatrapa	144
Dāmajadaśrī II	Son of Rudrasena I	Kṣatrapa	154-155
Vīradāman	Son of Dāmasena	Kṣatrapa	156-160
Yaśodāman	Son of Dāmasena	Mahākṣatrapa	160-161
Vijayasena	Son of Dāmasena	Kṣatrapa	161
		Mahākṣatrapa	161-172
Dāmajadaśrī III	Son of Dāmasena	Mahākṣatrapa	173-177
Rudrasena II	Son of Vīradāman	Mahākṣatrapa	177-198
Viśvasiṃha	Son of Rudrasena II	Kṣatrapa	197-200
Bhartṛdāman	Son of Rudrasena II	Kṣatrapa	200
		Mahākṣatrapa	204-217
Viśvasena	Son of Bhartṛdāman	Kṣatrapa	215-226

*Also spelt as Dāmaysada or Dāmaghsada

We know that the native Indian traditions give credit for founding the Śālivāhana Śaka era to Gautamīputra Śātakarṇi, so Chaṣṭana could not have founded this era. According to Indian traditions, the Śālivāhana Śaka era was founded to celebrate the uprooting of the Śakas, and thus it would not make sense to give a Śaka the credit for founding this era. We have two clues to fix the Kārdamaka Śaka chronology: the reference to a ruler named Tiastenes by Ptolemy, and the marriage of Kārdamaka Śaka ruler Rudradāman's daughter with a Sātavāhana ruler. Based on these two pointers, the revised chronology of Kārdamaka Śakas is presented in Table 8.4 along with the currently accepted chronology. The explanation for the proposed chronology is described below.

If we discount the possibility that Chaṣṭana founded the Śālivāhana Śaka era, then we are led to the conclusion that the Kārdamaka Śakas simply counted their regnal years from the date of ascension of their first ruler Chaṣṭana to the throne. Since we know that Chaṣṭana was ruling in year 52 of the era instituted by him, we know that he ruled for a long period. A rule of 52 years is not impossible if he started young and ruled till his seventies. He might have been forced to rule longer till his grandson came of age, as we know that his son did not rule possibly because of dying young. The question now is, when did Chaṣṭana start ruling?

Ptolemy wrote "Geographia" between 127-147 CE [11] and he has mentioned that Tiastenes was ruling Ozene (Ujjayinī) and Siriptolemaios (Śrī-Pulomāvi) was ruling Baithana (Pratiṣṭhāna) [12]. Modern historians consider Tiastenes to be a corrupt form of Chaṣṭana.

Table 8.4: Kārdamaka Śaka chronology

Kings	Years known	Modern Chronology [10]	Proposed Chronology
Chaṣṭana	52	130 CE	c. 100-152 CE
Jayadāman			Did not rule
Rudradāman	72	150 CE	c. 152-175 CE
Dāmajadaśrī			c. 175-200 CE
Jīvadāman	100-120	178-198 CE	c. 200-203 CE, c. 210-213 CE, c. 219-222 CE
Rudrasiṃha I	102-118	180-196 CE	c. 203-210 CE, c. 213-218 CE
Satyadāman			Ruled as Kṣatrapa
Rudrasena I	121-144	199-222 CE	c. 222-244 CE
Saṅghadāman	144-145	222-223 CE	c. 244-245 CE
Dāmasena	145-158	223-236 CE	c. 245-260 CE
Pṛthīvisena	144	222 CE	Ruled as Kṣatrapa
Dāmajadaśrī II	154-155	232-233 CE	Ruled as Kṣatrapa
Vīradāman	156-160	234-238 CE	Ruled as Kṣatrapa
Yaśodāman	160-161	238-239 CE	c. 260-261 CE
Vijayasena	161-172	239-250 CE	c. 261-273 CE
Dāmajadaśrī III	173-177	251-255 CE	c. 273-277 CE
Rudrasena II	177-198	255-276 CE	c. 277-300 CE
Viśvasiṃha	197-200	275-278 CE	Ruled as Kṣatrapa
Bhartṛdāman	200-217	278-295 CE	c. 300-326 CE
Viśvasena	215-226	293-304 CE	Ruled as Kṣatrapa

The data could have been collected many years earlier than the actual writing of Geographia. Looking at the proposed Sātavāhana chronology in Table 8.2, we can identify the Siriptolemaios (Śrī-Pulomāvi) mentioned by Ptolemy as Śivaśrī Pulumāvi, who ruled c. 113-120 CE. As Chaṣṭana was his contemporary, according to Ptolemy, he was also ruling during this period.

Chaṣṭana's grandson Rudradāman has claimed in the Junāgarh inscription that he defeated Śātakarṇi, Lord of Dakṣināpath (South India) twice, but did not kill him as he was a close relative. Based on the Kānheri inscription mentioning the marriage of a Kārdamaka Śaka princess to a Sātavāhana king, it can be concluded that Rudradāman's daughter was married to a Sātavāhana king named Śātakarṇi. Looking again at the proposed Sātavāhana chronology in Table 8.2, we can identify the Śātakarṇi, son-in-law of Rudradāman, as Chanḍaśrī Śātakarṇi, who ruled between 158-168 CE. This choice is necessitated by the fact that Rudradāman was the grandson of Chaṣṭana, contemporary of Śivaśrī Pulumāvi, and Śātakarṇi was married to the daughter of Rudradāman. Thus, there needs to be a considerable gap between Śivaśrī Pulumāvi, and Śātakarṇi, son-in-law of Rudradāman. As Chanḍaśrī Śātakarṇi was the penultimate ruler of the Sātavāhana dynasty, we can conclude that Sātavāhana Empire collapsed following the disastrous defeats suffered by Chanḍaśrī Śātakarṇi at the hands of his father-in-law Rudradāman. The Kārdamaka Śaka chronology presented in Table 8.4 is consistent with the points discussed above. It is estimated that Chaṣṭana ascended the throne in c. 100 CE and his descendants kept counting their regnal years from this date. We will conclude the discussion on Sātavāhanas here. We will now focus on the invaders that came from Central Asia.

Notes:

1. Sykes (1841). Quote on pages 426-427.
2. Maṇḍalik (1875).
3. Sahāya (1893).
4. Middleton (2015): 828.
5. Majumdar, Pusalker, and Majumdar (2001): 191-216.
6. Shastri (1999): 35.
7. Pargiter (1913): 36.
8. Pargiter (1913): 71-72.
9. Śrivāstava (2007): 298-299.
10. Majumdar, Pusalker, and Majumdar (2001): 178-190.
11. Waldman and Mason (2006): 374.
12. Sircar (1971): 227.

"History is dramatic license, covertly-financed with a sprinkling of gold dust from the newly-enthroned."

- Stewart Stafford

9. Invaders from Central Asia

Throughout history, India has seen invaders pour in through its western frontiers. Many of these invaders such as Kuṣāṇas came from Central Asia. The origin of Kuṣāṇas as described in modern history books is based on Chinese sources. The summary of the history of Kuṣāṇas is as follows [1]. Hiung-nu (the Huns) defeated Yué-Chi and drove them away around 200 BCE. As Hiung-nu continued to press down on the Yué-Chi, they broke into separate hordes. The lesser division, or "Little Yué-Chi," went to Tibet, while the "Great Yué-Chi's" moved first westwards and then in a southerly direction. Around 163 BCE, the Great Yué-Chi expelled the Śakas from Sogdiana, which was the land between the rivers Oxus and Jaxartes, north of Bactria. Sogdiana was the area around Samarkand in current day Uzbekistan. The displaced Śakas moved south to Bactria, the area around current day Balkh in northern Afghanistan. Around 120 BCE, the Great Yué-Chi started pouring into Bactria, and the expelled Śakas invaded India. At this point, the Yué-Chi consisted of five clans. Around 30 BCE, the Kwei-shuang clan subdued the rest of the clans and assumed sovereignty. The Yué-Chi then became known as Kwei-shuang or Kuṣāṇa.

It is an interesting story, but it may have nothing to do with the Kuṣāṇas. There are good reasons to believe that the Kuṣāṇas were of Turkish descent, and not Mongols. Bhandarkar has summarized the argument for Turkish descent of the Kuṣāṇas as follows:

> Kalhaṇa's Rājataraṅgiṇī speaks of Kanishka as sprung from the Turushka race which corresponds to the modern Turks. Again, Al Biruni tells us a legend which makes Kanika, i.e. Kanishka, a descendant of the Turk family called Shāhiya, founded by Barhatakīn, whom it describes as wearing "Turkish dress, a short tunic open in front, a high hat, boots and arms." And this is clearly attested by the royal figures on the coins, notably of Wema-Kadphises and Kanishka. About the costume and features of Wema-Kadphises, Kanishka's predecessor, H. H. Wilson makes the following remarks: "He wears a conical cap turned up at the sides, a tunic close to the body over which is a sort of strait coat: boots are invariably worn. The features are not those of the Mongal but of the Turk tribe." Thus Kalhan's statement, the legend mentioned by Al Biruni and the figures on the coins of Wema-Kadphises and Kanishka so thoroughly corroborate one another as to leave no doubt that in regard to the Turk extraction of Kanishka. [2]

Thus, from both literary and numismatic evidence, it stands to reason that the Kuṣāṇas were of Turkish descent.

9.1 The Kuṣāṇa Chronology

History books since the colonial times have been teaching that the Kuṣāna emperor Kaniṣka-I was the founder of the Śalivāhana Śaka era, which started in 78 CE. However, Kaniṣka was a Kuṣāna and not a Śaka. Modern historians have justified it by saying that the term Śaka was used by Indians for any foreigner. Recent research by Professor Harry Falk has demolished this theory. He has shown that according to the Yavanajātaka, by Sphujidhvaja, the Kuṣāna era started 149 years after the Śaka era, i.e. in 227 CE [3]. However, Falk has proposed the starting date of 127 CE by taking a hundred years off from this straightforward calculation with no ambiguity in the meaning of the text. The problem he faces in accepting the evidence of Yavanajātaka is that modern history has placed the Imperial Guptas in fourth century CE and the rule of the Kuṣāṇas has to end before the Imperial Guptas start ruling their territories. This makes the starting date of 227 CE for Kuṣāṇa era too late in the framework of currently accepted Indian chronology. In the chronological framework that I have developed, the time of the Imperial Guptas is several centuries before the Kuṣāṇas, and the Kuṣāṇa era can begin in 227 CE in accordance with the Yavanajātaka. Loeshner has considered three different starting dates for the accession of Kaniṣka I to the throne -- 78 CE, 127 CE, and 227 CE [4]. Table 9.1 shows the three versions of Kuṣāṇa chronology based on these three dates.

Table 9.1: Kuṣāṇa chronology [4]

	Modern chronology I *	**Modern chronology II****	**Modern chronology III*****
Kujula Kadphises	c. 20 BCE–20 CE	c. 20–60 CE	c. 50–125 CE
Wima Takto	c. 20 –55 CE	c. 60–95 CE	c. 125–180 CE
Wima Kadphises	c. 55–77 CE	c.95–126 CE	c. 180–226 CE
Kaniṣka I	77/78–c. 102 CE	126/127–152 CE	226/227–252 CE
Huviṣka	c. 102–142 CE	c.152–191 CE	c. 252–291 CE
Vasudeva I	c. 142–180 CE	c. 191–230 CE	291–330 CE
Kaniṣka II	c. 180–195 CE	c. 230–245 CE	c. 330–345 CE
Vasiṣka	c. 195–210 CE	c. 245–260 CE	c. 345–360 CE
Kaniṣka III	c. 210 –227 CE	c. 260–290 CE	c. 360–370 CE
Vasudeva II	c. 227–260 CE	c. 290–320 CE	c. 370–375 CE
Shaka	c. 260–295 CE	c. 320–355 CE	c. 375–390 CE
Kipunadha	c. 295 –320 CE	c. 355–375 CE	c. 390–400 CE

*Kuṣāṇa era starting in 78 CE
**Kuṣāṇa era starting in 127 CE
***Kuṣāṇa era starting in 227 CE

Modern chronology I is the version based on the assumption that the Kuṣāna emperor Kaniṣka-I was the founder of the Śalivāhana Śaka era. Modern chronology II has been gaining ground recently and is based on the work of Falk, who considers the Kuṣāna era to have begun in 127 CE with the accession of Kaniṣka-I. Modern chronology III has not become acceptable yet, though it gives the correct starting date of Kuṣāna era.

One of the important events to have taken place during the reign of Kaniṣka-I was the convening of the fourth Buddhist council in Kashmir [5]. Under the patronage of Kaniṣka-I, Buddhist monk Pārśva played an important role in organizing the Fourth Buddhist Council, in which 500 monks participated. As the council took place during the reign of Kaniṣka-I, it must have been during 227–252 CE. During this council the Buddhist scriptures were organized, and the great commentary on the Abhidharma was produced. Puruṣapura, current day Peshawar in Pakistan, was the main capital of Kaniṣka-I's vast empire, which extended from Bactria to Bihar. When Kaniṣka-I attacked and defeated the king of Magadha, he asked for a huge sum of money as indemnity, which the king of Magadha could not afford. Kaniṣka-I was instead offered a begging bowl used by the Buddha, and the services of Buddhist philosopher Aśvaghoṣa, which he accepted. Aśvaghoṣa then came to Puruṣapura with Kaniṣka-I and became his spiritual counsellor. Thus we can date Aśvaghoṣa to the second quarter of the third century CE.

Now that we are in the process of building the correct chronology of Indian history, we can explore the interactions between the sister civilizations of India and Persia to confirm the links that have been established by historians from pre-British era but denied by modern historians.

9.2 The Emperor of Persia

Ancient Indian and Persian civilizations were sister civilizations, both of them arising from the common source, the Indus Valley Civilization (IVC). When the

IVC cities became inhospitable around 1900 BCE, the Vedic Aryans migrated in different directions. Some clans moved east and south towards rest of India, while some other clans moved west towards Iran and then continued towards Europe. While Vedic Indians were able to completely preserve the Vedas due to their herculean effort unparalleled in history, ancient Persians were able to keep the Vedic wisdom more intact than the rest of Indo-European tribes due to their close proximity to the source of Vedic knowledge. Persians turned out to be great empire builders, and over time Persians had to face the same forces that tried to subjugate Indians as well. One of those deadly forces was the Hūṇas, who tried to overrun both of these civilizations. When the Kuṣāṇas were ruling Northwestern India, Persia was being ruled by the emperors of the Sasanian dynasty. According to Persian sources, Persian emperor Bahram had married an Indian princess during his visit to India [6-7]. The Indian princess was the daughter of Indian emperor Basdeo. There is not only literary but also numismatic proof to this effect from Persia as described below by Prinsep:

> One confirmation of a historical fact from numismatic aid has been remarked in the discovery of the name of Vāsa Deva or Bas Deo on a Sassanian coin. Ferishta states, that Bas Deo, of Kannauj, gave his daughter in marriage to Behram of Persia, A.D. 330:- the coin marks exactly such an alliance; but the Hindu chronicles admit no such name until, much later, one occurs in the Malwa catalogue of Abul Fazl. [8]

Prinsep again mentions this marriage in the genealogical table of Kanauj where he says that Basdeo (Vasudeva) revived the Kanauj dynasty and his daughter married Bahram Sassan of Persia in 390 CE, according to Ferishtah [9]. Fergusson has made the following comments in 1870 CE regarding the coins with Vasudeva written on one side and an image of a Sassanian king on other side:

> There is still another group of coins called Indo-Sassanian, which, however, have only been imperfectly read. The typical example of the class is one originally drawn by Prinsep, and produced by Thomas (vol. i, pl. vii., fig. 6.). It represents a Sassanian king on one side; on the other, another who may be an Indian with a distinctly legible inscription in Sanskrit characters, which reads Śrī Vasudeva. While the other inscriptions are undecyphered, it is too hazardous even to suggest that this may be the father-in-law of Bahram Gour; but the number of these Indo-Sassanian coins which are found in India, extending even beyond Hegira, prove a close intercourse between the two countries at the period we are now speaking about, and when thoroughly investigated, will, I fancy, throw more light on the political and religious changes that took place in India about the sixth century, than anything else which has yet come to light. [10]

The possibility of the marriage of an Indian princess, daughter of King Vasudeva, with Persian emperor Bahram is denied by modern Indian historians. There was no king named Basdeo in India when Bahram ruled in Persia, according to these historians. To show that this indeed was possible, I have compiled the list of rulers of Sasanian dynasty along with their regnal periods as shown in Table 9.2 [11]. To this, I have added the list of Kuṣāṇa monarchs along with their regnal periods according to Modern

Chronology III based on the accession of Kaniṣka-I to the throne in 227 CE (rightmost column in Table 9.1). Looking at this Table, we have to choose from a multitude of possibilities, instead of having no possibility at all. We have five Persian monarchs named Bahram and two Kuṣāṇa monarchs named Vasudeva, which is the equivalent of Basdeo in Persian stories.

Table 9.2: Sasanian and Kuṣāṇa chronology

Sasanian rulers	**Reign periods [11]**	**Kuṣāṇa rulers**	**Modern chronology III [4]**
Ardashir I	224–241 CE	Kujula Kadphises	c. 50–125 CE
Shapur I	241–272 CE	Wima Takto	c. 125– 180 CE
Hormizd I	272–273 CE	Wima Kadphises	c. 180–226 CE
Bahram I	273–276 CE	Kaniṣka I	226/227–252 CE
Bahram II	276–293 CE	Huviṣka	c. 252–291 CE
Bahram III	293 CE	Vasudeva I	291–350 CE
Narseh	293–302 CE	Kaniṣka II	c. 330–345
Hormizd II	302–309 CE	Vasiṣka	c. 345–360 CE
Shapur II the great	309–379 CE	Kaniṣka III	c. 360–370 CE
Ardashir II	379–383 CE	Vasudeva II	c. 370–375 CE
Shapur III	383–388 CE	Shaka	c. 375–390 CE
Bahram IV	388–399 CE	Kipunadha	c. 390–400 CE
Yazdegerd I	399–421 CE		
Bahram V	421–438 CE		

According to the Persian historians, it was Bahram V also known as Bahram Gor or Gūr, who married an Indian princess. It will then make Vasudeva II as the Indian emperor, who gave his daughter in marriage to Bahram Gor. Bahram Gor reigned between 421 to 438 CE, Vasudeva II ruled between c.370-375 CE according to

Modern Chronology III based on the accession of Kaniṣka-I to the throne in 227 CE. This brings the regnal period of Vasudeva II close to that of Bahram Gor, but there is a gap of about 45 years between the two rulers. Why do we have this gap, if the Persian traditions are so clear about the marriage alliance between Bahram Gor and Vasudeva II? To find the reason, we have to look at Table 9.1 again carefully.

Since Modern Chronology II is based on the accession of Kaniṣka-I to the throne in 127 CE and Modern Chronology III is based on the accession of Kaniṣka-I to the throne in 227 CE, one would expect a difference of 100 years between Modern Chronology II and Modern Chronology III. This clearly is not so for the last four rulers, and here is the reason. Modern historians have the Imperial Guptas reigning during the fourth and fifth century and therefore they are forced to wrap up the Kuṣāṇa dynasty before the Imperial Guptas have expanded into what is considered Kuṣāṇa territory. With no such restriction in the proposed chronology, the rule of later Kuṣāṇa rulers was later than shown in Modern Chronology III. Accordingly, it is entirely possible that Vasudeva II was still ruling when Bahram Gor visited India. In fact, we know this based on the numismatic evidence presented in this chapter. Based on this consideration, a revised chronology is proposed for Kuṣāṇa rulers starting with Kaniṣka-I as shown in Table 9.3, which affirms the marriage of Sasanian Emperor Bahram V with the daughter of Kuṣāṇa emperor Vasudeva II.

Table 9.3: Kuṣāṇa chronology

	Modern chronology II [4]	**Modern chronology III [4]**	**Proposed chronology**
	Kaniṣka era starting in 127 CE	Kaniṣka era starting in 227 CE	Kaniṣka era starting in 227 CE
Kaniṣka I	126/127-c. 152 CE	226/227–c. 252 CE	227–c. 252 CE
Huviṣka	c. 152–191 CE	c. 252–291 CE	c. 252–291 CE
Vasudeva I	191–c. 230 CE	291–c. 330 CE	291–c. 330 CE
Kaniṣka II	c. 230–c. 245 CE	c. 330–345 CE	c. 330–345 CE
Vasiṣka	c. 245–c.260 CE	c. 345–c. 360 CE	c. 345–c. 360 CE
Kaniṣka III	c. 260–c.290 CE	c. 360–c. 370 CE	c. 360–c.390 CE
Vasudeva II	c. 290–c. 320 CE	c. 370–c. 375 CE	c. 390–c. 435 CE
Shaka	c. 320–c. 355 CE	c. 375–c. 390 CE	c. 435–c. 455 CE
Kipunadha	c. 355–c. 375 CE	c. 390–c. 400 CE	c. 455–c. 475 CE

Kuṣāṇa were benign invaders who did not pose a threat to Indian civilization. However, after the Kuṣāṇas, India was invaded by hostile forces that severely wounded Indian civilization. Many Indian heroes rose to the challenges presented by these barbarian invaders. Out of those heroes, the Rajput clan of Sisodiyas shines the brightest. To trace their origins, we will need to reconsider the history of a celebrated kingdom called Vallabhī.

Notes:

1. Skrine (1899): 14-19.
2. Bhandarkar (1902).
3. Falk (2001).
4. Loeschner (2008).
5. Beal (1906): 151-152.
6. Analysis of Eastern Works (1838).
7. The Hindoos (1835): 327-329.
8. Thomas (1858): 221.
9. Thomas (1858): 258.
10. Fergusson (1870).
11. http://www.cais-soas.com/CAIS/History/Sasanian/sasanid.htm.

"Our greatest glory is not in never falling, but in rising every time we fall."
- Confucius

10. The Line of Blood

As North-west India fell to invaders, Vallabhī, a kingdom in present day Gujarat, became the beacon of hope for Hindu-Jain culture. A chain of events in the kingdom of Vallabhī brought into prominence the most celebrated clan of the Rajputs, the clan of Sisodias. The fascinating history of the rise of Sisodias has been denied by modern historians. Now is the time to reclaim the lost history of the ancestors of Sisodias, and in order to do that we need to establish the proper chronological framework of the history of Vallabhī.

Sisodias, who ruled from Mewar, belonged to the solar line of the kings and traced their ancestry to Lord Rama. They were the most exalted among the Rajput clans, and were called the "Sun of the Hindus" (Hindu Suraj). In this clan were born such great warriors and proud sons of the soil as Bappa Rawal, after whom the city of Rawalpindi in Pakistan is named, Maharana Pratap, and Kshatrapati Shivaji.

The fascinating story of the Sisodias begins with the arrival of Kanaksen, founder of this clan, to Saurashtra region in present day Gujarat in 145 CE, as described by Tod.

> At least ten genealogical lists, derived from the most opposite sources, agree in making Kanaksen the founder of this dynasty; and assign his emigration from the most northern of the provinces of India to the peninsula of Saurashtra in S. 201, or A.D. 145. [1]

Saurashtra was earlier named Surāṣṭra, meaning good country, from the prefix Su meaning good, and Rāṣṭra meaning country. The ancestors of Kanaksen had stayed at current day Lahore in Pakistan before Kanaksen moved to Dwarka in Saurashtra [2]. Vijayasen, a descendant of Kanaksen after four generations, rose to prominence and founded the celebrated city of Vallabhī [3].

10.1 The Official Genealogy

Sometime after Vijayasen, the kingdom was passed on to Bhaṭārka from whom the genealogy is commenced in the inscriptions of the rulers of Vallabhī. Alina copper plate inscription of Śilāditya VII gives the genealogy of Vallabhī rulers [4]. This inscription mentions that Guhasena was born in the line of Bhaṭārka. The son of Guhasena was Dhārasena (II), who was followed by his son Śīlāditya (I) Dharmāditya. He was followed by his younger brother Kharagraha (I), who was followed by his son Dharasena (III). Dharasena (III) was followed by his younger brother Dhruvasena (II) Bālāditya, who was followed by his son Dharasena (IV). Dharasena (IV) bore the imperial titles Paramabhattāraka, Mahārājādhirāja, Parameśvara, and Chakravartin. The kingdom then passed on to the line of Śilāditya (I), who was the (elder) brother of Kharagraha (I), grandfather of Dharasena (IV). Derabhaṭa was son of Śilāditya (I). Son of Derabhaṭa, Dhruvasena (III), became king next. He was followed by his elder brother Kharagraha

(II) Dharmāditya, who in turn was followed by his elder brother Śilāditya (II). After him the rule of Vallabhī passed from father to son successively in the following order: Śilāditya (III), Śilāditya (IV), Śilāditya (V), Śilāditya (VI) and Śilāditya (VII). All of these rulers bore imperial titles of Paramabhattāraka, Mahārājādhirāja, and Parameśvara.

Maliya copper plate inscription of Mahārāja Dharasena II of the year 252 provides the missing genealogy from Bhaṭārka to Guhasena [5]. There was illustrious Senāpati Bhaṭārka, whose son was Senāpati Dharasena (I). His younger brother was Mahārāja Droṇasingh, whose younger brother was Mahārāja Dhruvasena (I). Mahārāja Dharapaṭṭa was the younger brother of Mahārāja Dhruvasena (I). Son of Mahārāja Dharapaṭṭa was Mahārāja Guhasena, whose son was Mahārāja Dharasena (II).

10.2 Displaced in Time

The Alina copper plate inscription of Śilāditya VII was written in the year 447, which modern historians have taken to refer to the Vallabhī era. This has placed the last Vallabhī ruler Siladitya VII in 766 CE. This creates a peculiar situation that Bappa Rawal, who according to very well-established traditions was a descendant of Śilāditya (VII), was born before Śilāditya (VII) in the framework of modern chronology. The inscriptions of Vallabhī rulers specify only the year but not the era. It is discussed later in this chapter that Early Gurjaras, who were neighbours of Vallabhī rulers, used the Śaka era. It therefore stands to reason that Vallabhī rulers were also using the Śaka era.

Based on the assumption that Vallabhī rulers were using the Śaka era, Table 10.1 shows the proposed chronology of

Vallabhī rulers and compares with official chronology [4, 6-9]. I have added the names of Kanaksen and Vijayasen before Bhaṭārka as discussed earlier. Figure 10.1 shows the genealogy of the Vallabhī dynasty to illustrate the information presented in Table 10.1.

I have also added all the known years of the Vallabhī rulers that I have been able to find in the second column of Table 10.1 [10-12]. The inscriptions of Vallabhī rulers have not been compiled in a volume and many inscriptions have gone missing. There are only two inscriptions of the Vallabhī rulers in Volume 3 of the Corpus Inscriptionum Indicarum, which ideally should have contained all the inscriptions found till the date of its publication in 1888. This volume contains the inscriptions that used the Gupta/Vallabhī era in the editor's opinion. Many inscriptions of the Vallabhī rulers have not seen the light of day. Bhandarkar had written the following in 1872:

> Dr. Bhau Dāji gives, in one place, the dates of five copper plate grants of this dynasty, whilst in another he mentions seven dates professedly derived from copper plates. But he does not say when or by whom so many grants of the Vallabhī kings were discovered, nor who deciphered and translated them, or where the plates of their transcripts and translations are to be found. [13]

Table 10.1: Chronology of Vallabhī dynasty

Kings	**Years known**	**Accepted chronology**	**Proposed chronology**
Kanaksen			144 CE
Vijayasen			c. 204 CE
Bhaṭārka			c. 224 CE
Dharasena I			c. 244 CE
Droṇasingh		502 CE [10]	c. 261 CE
Dhruvasena I	207 [6], 216 [7]	525-545 CE	284-304 CE
Dharapaṭṭa			
Guhasena	240, 248 [8]	556-567 CE	315-326 CE
Dharasena II	252, 269, 270 [8]	571-590 CE	330-349 CE
Śilāditya I Dharmāditya	286 [8]	606-612 CE [10]	365-371 CE
Kharagraha		615 CE [11]	374 CE
Dharasena III		623 CE [12]	382 CE
Dhruvasena II Bālāditya	310 [8]	629-640 CE [11]	388-399 CE
Dharasena IV	326, 328, 330 [8]	645-650 CE	404-409 CE
Derabhaṭa			
Dhruvasena III	332 [8]	651 CE	410 CE
Kharagraha II Dharmāditya	337 [8]	656 CE	415 CE
Śilāditya II			
Śilāditya III Vajrāta	342[6], 348 [8], 352 [9], 356 [9]	662-684 CE [11]	420-443 CE
Śilāditya IV			
Śilāditya V	441 [8]	760 CE	519 CE
Śilāditya VI Dhrubhaṭa	447 [8]	766 CE	525 CE
Śilāditya VII	447 [4]	766 CE	525 CE

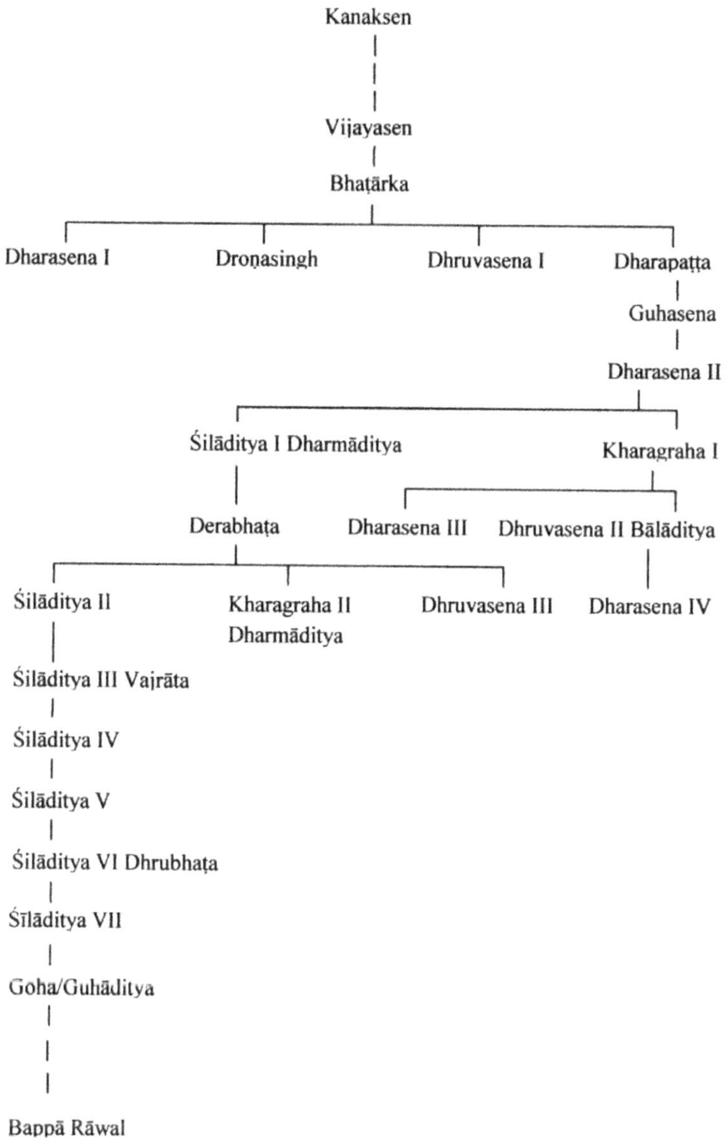

Figure 10.1: Genealogy of Vallabhī dynasty

Based on the reference provided by Bhandarkar, I have been able to find the set of five years mentioned by Bhāu Dāji on Vallabhī plates as 310, 332, 346, 347 and 376 [14]. It is certainly a matter of concern that some of these copper plates have simply vanished. It stands to reason that all inscriptions were vetted by British authorities and only those inscriptions have survived that in the eyes of the colonial authorities did not directly contradict the official chronology. If, somehow, some inscriptions escaped their attention and later proved to pose a challenge to the official chronology, these inscriptions were declared forgeries, as is the case of the Gurjara kings, who were neighbours of the Vallabhī kings.

10.3 The Gurjara Chronology

Gurjaras have a very special place in the history of India. The state of Gujarat, from where they originated, is named after them. One of their clans, the Pratihāras, defended India from invaders for many centuries. Currently, the early Gurjaras have been placed during the time period spanning from sixth to eighth century. The chronology of Gurjara kings is faulty because modern historians are dating the Gurjara inscriptions in the Chedi-Kalchuri era, while the inscriptions are in the Śaka era. There are three inscriptions of Gurjaras that explicitly mention the use of Śaka era [15]. These inscriptions are called Bagumrā, Umetā and Ilāo plate inscriptions. The establishment historians have declared these genuine inscriptions as forgeries [16-17]. The accepted and proposed chronologies of Gurjara rulers are shown in Table 10.2. Proposed chronology is based on using Śaka era for the Gurjara inscriptions.

Table 10.2: The Chronology of Early Gurjaras

Kings	Accepted dates [18]	Years known and Śaka equivalent	Proposed dates
Dadda (I)	570-595 CE		c. 410-435 CE
Jayabhaṭa (I) Vītarāga	595-620 CE		c. 435-455 CE
Dadda (II) Praśāntarāga	620-645 CE	380 (458 CE), 385 (463 CE), 392 (470 CE), 400 (478 CE), 415 (493 CE), 417 (495 CE)	c.455-500 CE
Jayabhaṭa (II)	645-665 CE		c. 500-505 CE
Dadda (III) Bāhusahāya	665-690 CE	427 (505 CE)	c. 505-525 CE
Jayabhaṭa (III)	690-715 CE	456 (534 CE), 460 (538 CE)	c. 525-540 CE
(Dadda (IV)) Ahirola	715-720 CE		c. 540-544 CE
Jayabhaṭa (IV)	720-738 CE	486 (564 CE)	c. 544-565 CE

The obvious problem with proposed chronology is the mention of Harṣadeva in the Gurjara inscriptions. Modern historians identify Harṣadeva with Harṣavardhana. According to the Nausāri inscription, a Gurjara ruler named Dadda protected a ruler of Vallabhī against the supreme lord (parameśvara) Śrīharṣadeva [15]. The point to note is that the Gurjara inscriptions do not explicitly mention Harṣavardhana. They only mention a king named Harṣa. He could not have been Harṣavardhana because Dadda II was the ruler of a small state. Dadda II was in no position to protect the Vallabhī king from Harṣavardhana, a mighty emperor who ruled over most of North India. This fact has been noted by all historians, including Bühler [15]. The Harṣadeva of the Gurjara inscriptions can be identified with Later Gupta king Harṣagupta.

According to the established chronology, Vallabhī rulers were issuing grants from the capital of Gurjara territory, while the Gurjaras at that point were independent rulers and did not have an overlord [15]. Dharasena IV was issuing grants from Broach, the capital of the Gurjaras, while the Gurjara ruler Dadda II called himself king of the kings. Of course, modern historians of India have found ways to explain away these inconvenient truths. In this case they have come up with the unsubstantiated theory that the Gurjaras had lost their sovereignty briefly when Dharasena IV issued grants from Broach. Well, it turns out that the ruler of Vallabhī was not the only one issuing grants from Gurjara territory, as the Chālukyas too were doing that [15]. If modern historians had the chronology right, these situations would not arise and they would not need to explain away the inconvenient facts. To show that the chronology developed in this book fits the known facts far better than the accepted chronology, I have prepared two Tables that are presented below. Table 10.3 shows selected Gurjara, Vallabhī and Chālukya rulers according to the accepted chronology.

Table 10.3: Gurjara, Vallabhī and Chālukya chronology: Accepted dates

Vallabhī [19]	**Gurjaras [18]**	**Chālukyas [20]**
Guhasena 556-567 CE	Dadda I 570-595 CE	Pulakeśina I 547-567 CE
Dharasena II 571-590 CE	Jayabhaṭa I Vītarāga 595-620 CE	Kirtivarman I 567-598 CE
Śilāditya I Dharmāditya 606-612 CE	Dadda II Praśāntarāga 620-645 CE	Mangaleśa 598-608 CE
Dhruvasena II Bālāditya 629-640 CE	Jayabhaṭa II 645-665 CE	Pulakeśina II 608-642 CE
Dharasena IV 645-650 CE	Dadda III Bāhusahāya 665-690 CE	Vikramāditya I 655-680 CE
Śilāditya III Vajrāta 662-684 CE	Jayabhaṭa III 690-715 CE	Vinayāditya 680-696 CE
Śilāditya IV-VI 685-766 CE	(Dadda IV) Ahirola 715-720 CE	Vijayāditya 696-733 CE
Śilāditya VII 766 CE	Jayabhaṭa IV 720-738 CE	Vikramāditya II 733-743 CE

According to Table 10.3, when Dharasena IV was issuing grants from Broach, Gurjara king Jayabhaṭa II was ruling. His father Dadda II had already declared himself the king of kings, so starting from Dadda II, Gurjara rulers were sovereign and would not allow anyone to issue grants from their capital. The same argument applies to Chālukya rulers issuing grants from Gurjara territory.

Table 10.4 shows selected Gurjara, Vallabhī and Chālukya rulers according to the proposed chronology. Please note that ruling periods of the Chālukya rulers stay the same in both Tables as the Chālukya rulers have specified their dates in Śaka era, which makes their dating unequivocal. If we look at Table 10.4 carefully, we will find that contradictions listed above do not arise when we have the correct chronology. When Dharasena IV was issuing grants from Broach, Gurjara kings had not even started their rule. When Chālukya rulers were issuing grants from supposedly Gurjara territory, the rule of Gurjara kings had already come to an end.

Table 10.4: Gurjara, Vallabhī and Chālukya chronology: Proposed dates (Gurjara and Vallabhī)

Vallabhī	**Gurjaras**	**Chālukyas [20]**
Guhasena 315-326 CE	Dadda I c. 410-435 CE	Pulakeśina I 547-567 CE
Dharasena II 330-349 CE	Jayabhaṭa I Vītarāga c. 435-455 CE	Kirtivarman I 567-598 CE
Śilāditya I Dharmāditya 365-371 CE	Dadda II Praśāntarāga c. 455-500 CE	Mangaleśa 598-608 CE
Dhruvasena II Bālāditya 388-399 CE	Jayabhaṭa II c. 500-505 CE	Pulakeśina II 608-642 CE
Dharasena IV 404-409 CE	Dadda III Bāhusahāya c. 505-525 CE	Vikramāditya I 655-680 CE
Śilāditya III Vajrāta 420-443 CE	Jayabhaṭa III c. 525-540 CE	Vinayāditya 680-696 CE
Śilāditya IV-VI 444-525 CE	(Dadda IV) Ahirola c. 540-544 CE	Vijayāditya 696-733 CE
Śilāditya VII 525-543 CE	Jayabhaṭa IV c. 544-565 CE	Vikramāditya II 733-743 CE

When we look at Table 10.4 closely, we find something fascinating. The rise of the early Gurjaras coincides with the change in guard at Vallabhī. We know from the inscriptions of the Vallabhī rulers that after Dharasena IV, the throne of the Vallabhī suddenly went to the bloodline of

Śilāditya I Dharmāditya, who was the brother of the Kharagraha I, grandfather of Dharasena IV. The rule of Vallabhī never went back to the line of Dharasena IV. There are two possibilities here. Either there was an attack by the invaders, possibly Hūṇas, or there was an internal struggle for power. The result was the transfer of power to Śilāditya II. The Gurjara ruler Dadda I helped Śilāditya II in gaining control of power and was rewarded by being made a sub-ordinate ruler. The relations between Gurjara rulers and Vallabhī rulers remained cordial based on this mutual gratitude.

When the Later Gupta king Harṣagupta attacked Vallabhī, it was only natural for the Gurjara ruler Dadda II to come to the rescue of his overlord at that point in time. The Vallabhī ruler, who was attacked by Harṣagupta, would be either Śilāditya V or VI. As a token of gratitude, Dadda II was accepted as a sovereign ruler by the Vallabhī king, and Dadda II assumed the title of the king of the kings.

There was peace and prosperity in Vallabhī after the attack by the later Gupta king Harṣagupta, until one day it was sacked by the invaders from Central Asia.

10.4 The Sacking of Vallabhī

The last known ruler of Vallabhī was Śilāditya VII, as per the inscriptions. According to well-established traditions of the Sisodias, Vallabhī was sacked during the reign of Śilāditya. The sacking of Vallabhī is described by Tod [21] in these words:

> And a work written to commemorate the reign of Rana Raj Singh opens with these words: 'In the west is Sorathdes, a country well known: the barbarians invaded

> it, and conquered Bal-ka-nath; all fell in the sack of Valabhipura, except the daughter of the Pramara.' And the Sandrai roll thus commences: 'When the city of Valabhi was sacked, the inhabitants fled and founded Bali, Sandrai, and Nadol in Mordar des.' These are towns yet of consequence, and in all the Jain religion is still maintained, which was the chief worship of Valabhipura when sacked by the 'barbarian.' The records preserved by the Jains give S.B. 205 (A.D. 524) as the date of this event. ... One of the poetic chronicles thus commences: 'The barbarians had captured Gajni. The house of Siladitya was left desolate. In its defence his heroes fell; of his seed but the name remained.' [21]

As the tradition remembers Śilāditya as the ruler when Vallabhī was sacked, and the last named ruler of Vallabhī based on the inscriptions was Śilāditya VII, we can safely conclude that Vallabhī was sacked during the rule of Śilāditya VII. There is an interesting legend about Śilāditya that tries to explain why Śilāditya lost to the invaders:

> There was a fountain (Suryakunda) 'sacred to the sun' at Valabhipura, from which arose at the summons of Siladitya (according to the legend) the seven-headed horse Saptasva, which draws the car of Surya, to bear him to battle. With such an auxiliary no foe could prevail; but a wicked minister revealed to the enemy the secret of annulling this aid, by polluting the sacred fountain with blood. This accomplished, in vain did the prince call on Saptasva to save him from the strange and barbarous foe: the charm was broken, and with it sunk the dynasty of Valabhi. [22]

As quoted above, Jain traditions maintain that Vallabhī was sacked in 524 CE. If we assume that Vallabhī rulers were using the Śaka era, the last known date of Śilāditya VII would fall in 525 CE as shown in Table 10.1. These two dates differ by only one year, which is quite tantalizing. Thus, the assumption that Vallabhī rulers were using the Śaka era is in line with well-established traditions. Obviously, there will be objection to this thesis by the modern historians.

10.5 Mistaken Identities

According to modern historians, the Vallabhī king Dhruvasena II Bālāditya was married to the daughter of emperor Harṣavardhana. This is based on the testimony of Xuan Zang (Hiuen Tsiang). How is this possible in the proposed chronology where we show that Dhruvasena II Bālāditya was ruling towards the end of fourth century CE and Harṣavardhana ruled in the first half of the seventh century CE? In fact, there is no proof that the name of the Vallabhī ruler who was married to the daughter of emperor Harṣavardhana was Dhruvasena or Bālāditya. To prove that we need to know exactly the name that Hiuen Tsiang has mentioned. This information is provided by Bühler as follows:

> The remarks of Hiuen Tsiang leave no doubt that it was Dhruvasena II, who had to fly before the armies of the great king of Kanauj. He says, Siyuki, II. p. 267 (Beal), in his account of Valabhi, "the present king is of the Kshatriya caste, as they all are. He is the nephew of Śilāditya rāja of Mālava, and son-in-law of the son of Śilāditya [i.e. Śrīharsha] the present king of Kanyākubja. His name is Dhruvabhaṭa (Tu-lu-ho-po-tu). He is of a lively and hasty disposition, his wisdom and state-craft are shallow. [23]

The name given by Hiuen Tsiang of the Vallabhī king married to the daughter of emperor Harṣavardhana was "Tu-lu-ho-po-tu". How did modern historians come to the conclusion that "Tu-lu-ho-po-tu" is Dhruvabhaṭa? They did so simply by checking who was ruling Vallabhī during the time of Harṣavardhana, according to the accepted chronology. Since the last part of the name of Dhruvasena didn't sound anywhere close to the last part of "Tu-lu-ho-po-tu", they changed the name of Dhruvasena to Dhruvabhaṭa. If we look at it objectively, there is no similarity between "Tu-lu-ho-po-tu" and Dhruvasena or Dhruvabhaṭa. In fact, we can challenge these historians and ask them why neither Dhruvasena II Bālāditya nor any of his successors mention that Dhruvasena II Bālāditya was married to the daughter of emperor Harṣavardhana. They should have been happy about it, but they fail to mention it even once though they continued to rule for more than a century after this supposed marriage had taken place. Modern historians have developed this fancy theory that Harṣavardhana first attacked the Vallabhī king, who was protected by Dadda II backed by Pulakeshina II, but later Harṣavardhana changed his mind and got his daughter married to Vallabhī king [24]. There is no proof of Pulakeshina II backing Dadda II. In the chronology developed in this book, they were not even contemporaries. Due to the application of wrong eras to years mentioned in inscriptions, the true history of India has been muddled and its true heroes have been denied their due places in history. The biggest contribution to preserving the culture of ancient India came from a bloodline that has its origins in the kingdom of Vallabhī.

10.6 The bloodline

The royal line of Vallabhī was all but wiped out along with multitudes of its people when Vallabhī was sacked by barbarians, but as luck would have it, the son of Śilāditya VII was safe, far away from Vallabhī. Let us continue with what happened after the sacking of Vallabhī by the barbarians:

> Of the prince's family, the queen Pushpavati alone escaped the sack of Valabhi, as well as the funeral pyre, upon which, on the death of Siladitya, his other wives were sacrificed. She was a daughter of the Pramara prince of Chandravati, and had visited the shrine of the universal mother, Amba-Bhavani, in her native land, to deposit upon the altar of the goddess a votive offering consequent to her expectation of offspring. She was on her return, when the intelligence arrived which blasted all her future hopes, by depriving her of her lord, and robbing him, whom the goddess had just granted to her prayers, of a crown. Excessive grief closed her pilgrimage. Taking refuge in a cave in the mountains of Malia, she was delivered of a son. Having confided the infant to a Brahmani of Birnagar named Kamlavati, enjoining her to educate the young prince as a Brahman, but to marry him to a Rajputni, she mounted the funeral pile to join her lord. Kamlavati, the daughter of the priest of the temple, was herself a mother, and she performed the tender offices of one to the orphan prince, whom she designated Goha, or 'cave-born.' The child was a source of perpetual uneasiness to its protectors: he associated with Rajput children, killing birds, hunting wild animals, and at the age of eleven was totally unmanageable: to use the words of the legend, "How should they hide the ray of the sun?"

At this period Idar was governed by a chief of the savage race of Bhil; his name, Mandalika. The young Goha frequented the forests in company with the Bhils, whose habits better assimilated with his daring nature than those of the Brahmans. He became a favourite with the Vanaputras, or 'children of the forest,' who resigned to him Idar with its woods and mountains. The fact is mentioned by Abu-l Fazl, and is still repeated by the bards, with a characteristic version of the incident, of which doubtless there were many. The Bhils having determined in sport to elect a king, the choice fell on Goha; and one of the young savages, cutting his finger, applied the blood as the tika of sovereignty to his forehead. What was done in sport was confirmed by the old forest chief. The sequel fixes on Goha the stain of ingratitude, for he slew his benefactor, and no motive is assigned in the legend for the deed. Goha's name became the patronymic of his descendants, who were styled Guhilot, classically Grahilot, in time softened to Gehlot.

We know very little concerning these early princes but that they dwelt in this mountainous region for eight generations; when the Bhils, tired of a foreign rule, assailed Nagaditya, the eighth prince, while hunting, and deprived him of life and Idar. The descendants of Kamlavati (the Birnagar Brahmani), who retained the office of priest in the family, were again the preservers of the line of Valabhi. The infant Bappa, son of Nagaditya, then only three years old, was conveyed to the fortress of Bhander, where he was protected by a Bhil of Yadu descent. Thence he was removed for greater security to the wilds of Parasar. Within its impervious recesses rose the three-peaked (trikuta) mountain, at whose base was the town of Nagindra, the

> abode of Brahmans, who performed the rites of the 'great god.' In this retreat passed the early years of Bappa, wandering through these Alpine valleys, amidst the groves of Bal and the shrines of the brazen calf. [25]

Thus, according to well-established traditions, it is clear that the great Bappa Rawal was a direct descendant of Śilāditya VII and was separated from him by eight generations. It will be appropriate at this point then to make a few remarks regarding the chronology of Vallabhī rulers. Modern historians have used Vallabhī era to date the Vallabhī inscriptions, which makes Śilāditya VII rule in the year 766 CE. This has completely muddied the well-preserved traditions of Mewar and the genealogy maintained by the Rajputs. Currently, Bappa Rawal is dated to 713-753 CE making him anterior to his ancestor Śilāditya VII. It was Bappa Rawal, who protected India from Arab invasion and pursued the invaders deep into their territories. When India finally fell to invaders, it was his descendants like Maharana Pratap and Kshatrapati Shivaji, who kept on fighting the invaders. It was due to the unparalled bravery and sacrifices of Bappa Rawal's bloodline that ancient Indian civilization survived the longest and most barbaric persecution known in history.

When time permits, I hope to narrate the exploits of Bappa Rawal and the subsequent history of India in my book "India after Bappa Rawal: Dark Horizons."

Notes

1. Tod (1920): 251.
2. Tod (1920): 252.

3. Tod (1920): 253.
4. Fleet (1888): 171-191.
5. Fleet (1888): 164-171.
6. Bühler (1876).
7. Bühler (1875).
8. Bühler (1878).
9. Bühler (1882).
10. Majumdar, Pusalker, and Majumdar (1997): 60-63.
11. Agnihotry (2010): A-416.
12. Śrivāstava (2007): 452-453.
13. Bhandarkar (1872).
14. Dāji (1872).
15. Bühler (1888).
16. Mirashi (1955): 57-66.
17. Mirashi (1955): 67-72.
18. Mirashi (1955): cxc.
19. See Table 10.1.
20. Daniélou (2003): 155-159.
21. Tod (1920): 253-255.
22. Tod (1920): 257.
23. Bühler (1888).
24. Mirashi (1955): lii-liii.
25. Tod (1920): 258-260.

Bibliography

Agnihotry, V. K. (Chief Editor) (2010). Indian History. 26th edition. Mumbai, India: Allied publishers.

Analysis of Eastern Works – No. 1 - The Rozat al Sofa. (1838). The Asiatic Journal and Monthly Register for British and Foreign India, China and Australasia – New Series, Vol. XXVI: 228-237.

Anson, E. M. (2013). Alexander the Great: Themes and issues. London, UK: Bloomsbury Academic.

Bakshi, S. R. and Ralhan, O. P. (editors). (2007). Madhya Pradesh Through the Ages. Volume 3. Delhi, India: Sarup and Sons.

Basham, A.L. (1951). History and doctrines of the Ājīvikas: A vanished Indian religion. Delhi, India: Motilal Banarasidass.

Basham, A.L. (1982). Aśoka and Buddhism – A Reexamination. The Journal of the International Association of Buddhistic Studies, 5 (1): 131-143.

Beal, S. (1884). Si-Yu-Ki: Buddhist Records of the Western World, Volume I. London, UK: Trubner and Co.

Beal, S. (1906). Si-Yu-Ki: Buddhist Records of the Western World, Volume I. London, UK: Kegan Paul, Trench, Trubner and Co Ltd.

Bernholz, P. and Valubel, R. (Editors). (2014). Explaining Monetary and Financial Innovation: A Historical Analysis. Switzerland: Springer International.

Bhandarkar, R.G. (1872). A Tāmba Patra or Ancient Copper Plate Grant from Kāthiāwād. Indian Antiquary, 1: 14-18.

Bhandarkar, D. R. (1902). A Kushana Stone Inscription and the Question about the Origin of the Śaka Era. The Journal of the Bombay Branch of the Royal Asiatic Society, 20: 269-302.

Bühler, G. (1875). A grant of King Dhruvasena I of Valabhi. The Indian Antiquary. 4: 104-106.

Bühler, G. (1876). Grants from Valabhi. The Indian Antiquary, 5: 204-212.

Bühler, G. (1878). Additional Valabhi Grants, Nos. IX-XIV. The Indian Antiquary, 7: 66-86.

Bühler, G. (1882). Valabhi Grants. The Indian Antiquary, 11: 305-309.

Bühler, G. (1888). Gurjara Inscriptions, No. III: A New Grant of Dadda II or Prasantaraga. The Indian Antiquary, 17: 183-201.

Charpentier, J. (1931). Antiochus, King of the Yavanas. Bulletin of the School of Oriental Studies, 6 (2): 303-321.

Chatterjee, S. (1998). Indian Civilization and Culture. New Delhi, India: M D Publications Pvt Ltd.

Chinnock, E. J. (1884). The Anabasis of Alexander. London, UK: Hodder and Stoughton.

Dājī, B. (1861). On the Sanskrit Poet, Kālidāsa. Journal of the Bombay Branch of the Royal Asiatic Society, 21: 19-30.

Dāji, B. (1872). The ancient Sanskrit Numerals in the Cave Inscriptions, and on Sah-coins, correctly made out; with remarks on the era of Śālivāhana and Vikramāditya. Journal of Bombay Branch of Royal Asiatic Society, 8: 225-233.

Daniélou, A. (2003). A brief history of India. Rochester, Vermont, USA: Inner Traditions International.

Davids, T. W. R. (1877). International Numismata Orientalia: On the Ancient Coins and Measures of Ceylon. London, UK: Trubner & Co.

Dietz, S. (1995). The Dating of the Historical Buddha in the History of Western Scholarship up to 1980. In "When Did the Buddha Live? The Controversy on the Dating of the Historical Buddha", edited by Heinz Bechert." Delhi, India: Sri Satguru Publications.

Duncker, M. (1880). The History of Antiquity. Volume 4. London, UK: Richard Bentley & Son.

Eggermont, P.H.L. (1968). The Purāṇa source of Merutuṅga's list of kings and the arrival of Śakas in India" in Papers on the Date of Kaniṣka, edited by A.L. Basham. Leiden, Netherlands: E.J. Brill.

Falk, H. (2001). The yuga of Sphujiddhvaja and the era of the Kuṣāṇas. Silk Road Art and Archaeology, 7, 121-136.

Fergusson, J. (1870). Art. II. – On Indian Chronology. Journal of the Royal Asiatic Society of Great Britain and Ireland, New Series, Volume the Fourth: 81-137.

Fergusson, J. (1876). History of Indian and Eastern Architecture. London, UK: John Murray.

Fleet, J. F. (1888). Corpus Inscriptionum Indicarum, Vol. III: Inscriptions of the Early Guptas. Calcutta, India: Government of India, Central Publications Branch.

Goonetilleke, W. (1884). The Navaratna. The Orientalist, 1: 97-109.

Gopal, R. (1984). Kālidāsa: His Art and Culture. New Delhi, India: Concept Publishing Company.

Goyala, S. (1987a). Gupta Sāmrājya kā Itihāsa (in Hindi). Meerut, U.P., India: Kusumāñjali Prakāśana.

Goyala, S. (1987b). Samudragupta Parākramāṅka (in Hindi). Meerut, U.P., India: Kusumāñjali Prakāśana.

Hamilton, H.C. (1892). The Geography of Strabo. Volume 1. London, UK: George Bell and Sons.

Hultzsch, E. (1914). The Date of Aśoka. Journal of the Royal Asiatic Society of Great Britain and Ireland, October: 943-951.

Hultzsch, E. (1925). Corpus Inscriptionum Indicarum, Vol. I: Inscriptions of Asoka. New Edition. Oxford, UK: Printed for the Government of India at the Clarendon Press.

Jain, K. C. (1972). Malwa Through the Ages. New Delhi, India: Motilal Banarsidass.

Jain, K. C. (1991). Lord Mahāvīra and his times. New Delhi, India: Motilal Banarsidass.

Jayaswal, K.P. (1934). An Imperial History of India in a Sanskrit Text. Revised by Rahula Sankrityayana. Lahore, United India: Motilal Banarsi Dass.

Jones, W. (1788). On the Chronology of the Hindus. Asiatick Researches or Transactions of the Society Instituted in Bengal, 2: 111-147 (1807 reprint).

Jones, W. (1793). The Tenth Anniversary Discourse. Asiatick Researches or Transactions of the Society Instituted in Bengal, 4: xii-xiv.

Loeschner, H. (2008). Notes on the Yuezhi – Kushan relationship and Kushan chronology. Oriental Numismatic Society: 1-28.

Majumdar, R. C. (1977). Ancient India. Eighth Edition. Delhi, India: Motilal Banarasidass.

Majumdar, R. C. and Altekar, A. S. (editors). (1967). The Vakataka-Gupta Age. , Delhi, India: Motilal Banarasidass.

Majumdar, R.C., Pusalker, A.D. and Majumdar A.K. (Editors). (1997). The History and Culture of the Indian People, Volume III: The Classical Age. 5th Edition. Mumbai, India: Bharatiya Vidya Bhavan.

Majumdar, R.C., Pusalker, A.D. and Majumdar A.K. (Editors). (2001). The History and Culture of the Indian People, Volume II: The Age of Imperial Unity. 7th Edition. Mumbai, India: Bharatiya Vidya Bhavan.

Malla, K. P. (2005). Manadeva Samvat: An investigation into an Historical Fraud. Contributions to Nepalese Studies, 32 (1): 1-49.

Maṇḍalik, R. S. V. N. (1875). Art. XII. – Śālivāhana and Śālivāhana Saptaśatī. The Journal of the Bombay Branch of the Royal Asiatic Society, 10: 127-138.

McCrindle, J. W. (1877). Ancient India as Described by Megasthenes and Arrian. London, UK: Trubner & Co.

McCrindle, J. W. (1893). The Invasion of India by Alexander the Great. Westminster, UK: Archibald Constable and Co.

McCrindle, J. W. (1901). Ancient India as Described in Classical Literature. Westminster, UK: Archibald Constable and Co.

Middleton, J. (2015). World monarchies and dynasties. New York, USA: Routledge.

Mirashi, V.V. (editor). (1955). Corpus Inscriptionum Indicarum, Vol. IV: Inscriptions of the Kalachuri-Chedi era. Part 1. New Delhi, India: Archaeological Survey of India.

Mirashi, V.V. (editor). (1963). Corpus Inscriptionum Indicarum, Vol. V, Inscriptions of the Vākāṭakas. New Delhi, India: Archaeological Survey of India.

Mirashi, V.V. (1974). Bhavabhūti: His Date, Life, and Works. Delhi, India: Motilal Banarsidass.

Monier-Williams, M. (1988). Sanskrit-English dictionary. Third reprint. New Delhi, India: Munshiram Manoharlal.

Mookerji, R., (1973). The Gupta Empire. Fifth Edition. New Delhi, India: Motilal Banarsidass.

Mukhopadhyaya, S. (1963). The Aśokavadana. Delhi, India: Sahitya Akademi.

Nirmala, R. (1992). Anādi Ujjayinī (in Hindi). Mumbai, India: Anviti Prakāśana.

Olivelle, P. (Editor). (2006). Between the Empires: Society in India 300 BCE to 400 CE. New York, USA: Oxford University Press.

Pandey, R. B., (1951). Vikramāditya of Ujjayinī. Banaras, India: Shatadala Prakashana.

Pargiter, F. E. (1913). The Purana Text of the Dynasties of the Kali Age. London, UK: Humphrey Milford and Oxford University Press.

Penzer, N.M. (editor) (1928). The Ocean of Story: Being C.H. Tawney's translation of Somadeva's Katha Sarit Sagara. Volume 9. London, UK: Chas. J. Sawyer Ltd.

Prinsep, J. (1837). Interpretation of the most ancient of the inscriptions on the pillar called the lat of Feroz Shah, near Delhi, and of the Allahabad, Radhia and Mattiah pillar, or lat, inscriptions which agree therewith. Journal of Royal Asiatic Society of Bengal, July: 566-609.

Prinsep, J. (1838a). Discovery of the name of Antiochus the Great, in two of the edicts of Aśoka, king of India. Journal of Royal Asiatic Society of Bengal, February: 156-167.

Prinsep, J. (1838b). On the edicts of Piyadasi, or Aśoka, the Buddhist monarch of India, preserved on the Girnar rock in the Gujerat peninsula, and on the Dhauli rock in Cuttack; with the discovery of Ptolemy's name therein. Journal of Royal Asiatic Society of Bengal, March: 219-282.

Rost, R. (editor) (1865). Essays: Analytical, Critical and Philological on the subjects connected with Sanskrit literature by the late H.H. Wilson. Volume 3. London, UK: Trubner & Co.

Roy, R.R.M. (2020). Zero Point of Jain Astronomy: The Origin of Malava Era. Mississauga, Ontario, Canada: Mount Meru Publishing.

Sahāya, P. J. (1893). The Samvat Era. The Imperial and Asiatic Quarterly Review, New Series, 5 (9-10): 363-369.

Saloman, R. (1989). New Inscriptional Evidence for the History of the Aulikaras of Mandasor. Indo-Iranian Journal, 32: 1-36.

Sen, S. N. (1999). Ancient Indian History and Civilization. Second Edition. New Delhi, India: New Age International Publishers.

Sethna, K. D. (1989). Ancient India in a New Light. New Delhi, India: Aditya Prakashana.

Shastri, A.M. (1996). Vikrama era, Indian Journal of History of Science, 31(1): 35-65.

Shastri, A.M. (Editor). (1999). The Age of the Satavahanas. Vol. I. New Delhi, India: Aryan Books International.

Sircar, D.C. (1969). Ancient Malwā and the Vikramāditya Tradition. Delhi, India: Munshiram Manoharlal.

Sircar, D.C. (1971). Studies in the Geography of Ancient and Medieval India. Second Edition. Delhi, India: Motilal Banarsidass.

Skrine, F. H. (1899). The Heart of Asia: A History of Russian Turkestan and the Central Asian Khanates from the Earliest Times. London, UK: Methuen & Co.

Śrivāstava, K.C. (2007). Prāchina Bhārata kā Itihāsa tathā Sanskṛti (in Hindi). 11th edition. Allahabad, India: United Book Depot.

Strong, J. S. (1989). The legend of King Aśoka: A study and translation of the Aśokavadana. Delhi, India: Motilal Banarsidass.

Subba Reddy, V.V. (2009). Temples of south India. New Delhi, India: Gyan publishing House.

Sykes, W. H. (1841). Art. XIV.—Notes on the Religious, Moral, and Political State of India, before the Mahomedan Invasion, chiefly founded on the Travels of the Chinese Buddhist Priest, Fa Hian, in India, A.D. 399, and on the Commentaries of Messrs. Remusat, Klaproth, Burnouf, and Landresse. Journal of the Royal Asiatic Society of Great Britain and Ireland, 6: 248-450.

Thapar, R. (2013). The Past before us. Cambridge, Massachusetts, USA: Harvard University Press.

The Hindoos. Volume II. (1835). London, UK: Charles Knight.

Thomas, E. (1858). Essays on Indian Antiquities, historic, Numismatic, and Paleographic of the late James Prinsep to which are added his Useful Tables, illustrative of Indian history, chronology, modern coinage, weights, measures, etc. Volume II. London, UK: John Murray.

Tod, J. (1920). Annals and Antiquities of Rajasthan or the Central and Western Rajput States of India. Edited with an introduction and notes by William Crooke. Volume 1 (Original Dedication of the First Volume: June 20, 1829). Oxford, UK: Oxford University Press.

Vassilkov, Y. V. (1997-98). On the meaning of the names Aśoka and Piyadasi. Indologica Taurinensia, 23-24: 441-457.

Venkatachelam, K. (1953). The plot in Indian Chronology. Ghandhinagara/Vijayawada, India: Bharata Charitra Bhaskara.

Venkatachelam, K. (1956). Age of Buddha, Milinda & Amtiyoka and Yugapurana. Ghandhinagara/Vijayawada, India: Bharata Charitra Bhaskara.

Vyāsaśiṣya, K. (1988). Puranon men Itihasa (in Hindi). Delhi, India: Itihasa Vidya Prakashana.

Waldman, C. and Mason, C. (2006). Encyclopedia of European Peoples. New York, USA: Facts on File, Inc.

Wilford, C. (1809a). Essay III: Of the kings of Magadha; their chronology. Asiatic Researches, 9: 82-116.

Wilford, C. (1809b). Essay IV: Vicramaditya and Salivahana. Asiatic Researches, 9: 117-243.

Willis, M. (2005). Later Gupta History: Inscriptions, Coins and Historical Ideology. Journal of the Royal Asiatic Society, Third Series, 15(2), 131-150.

Wilson, H. H. (1850). On the Rock Inscription of Kapur Di Giri, Dhauli, and Girnar. The Journal of the Royal Asiatic Society of Great Britain and Ireland, Volume the Twelfth: 153-251.

Index

Also by Mount Meru Publishing

Author: Dr. Raja Ram Mohan Roy

1. Vedic Physics: Scientific Origin of Hinduism
2. India before Alexander: A New Chronology
3. India after Alexander: The Age of Vikramādityas
4. India after Vikramāditya: The Melting Pot
5. Zero Points of Vedic Astronomy: Discovery of the Original Boundaries of Nakshatras
6. Zero Point of Jain Astronomy: The Origin of Mālava Era

Author: Professor Subhash Kak

1. The Circle of Memory: An Autobiography
2. Matter and Mind: The Vaisheshika Sutra of Kanada
3. Arrival and Exile: Selected Poems
4. Computation in Ancient India
5. Mind and Self: Patanjali's Yoga Sutra and Modern Science
6. The Nature of Physical Reality (Third Edition)

Author: Dr. Dilip Amin

1. Interfaith Marriage: Share and Respect with Equality

Author: Professor Ramesh Rao

1. The Election that Shaped Gujarat and Narendra Modi's Rise to National Stardom

About the Author

I am a seeker in search of the true history and heritage of India. I have strong scientific background (B.Tech. in Metallurgical Engineering from Indian Institute of Technology, Kanpur and Ph.D. in Materials Science and Engineering from The Ohio State University, USA) and a deep interest in ancient Indian texts. My work on Indology spans three different fields: cosmology, astronomy, and history. My first book "Vedic Physics: Scientific Origin of Hinduism" details the cosmological framework in which the Ṛgveda, first book of humankind, is to be understood. Anyone who has read the Ṛgveda with an open mind will know that the book does not make sense if taken literally as it is full of rich symbols. Many of these symbolic and mysterious sounding passages start to make perfect sense in the light of my discovery of the Ṛgveda as a coded book of cosmology.

My in-depth work on Hindu astronomy enabled by my science background led me to realize that if great Indian astronomer Varāhmihira is placed in 6th century CE as stipulated by many Indic scholars, both western and some Indian, then that essentially means that the boundaries of sidereal Hindu and western zodiacs do not match and have a difference of about 10°. The search for the origin of this discrepancy led me to reassess the boundaries of nakṣatras and identifications of yogatārās. In my book "Zero Points of Vedic Astronomy: Discovery of the Original Boundaries of Nakshatras" I show that the original boundary of Aświnī nakṣatra is at 8° from Hamal or 10° from Revatī. This crucial discovery synchronizes the sidereal Hindu and western zodiacs.

My book "Zero Point of Jain Astronomy: The Origin of Mālava Era" addresses the important question of the origin of Mālava Era. Jain astronomy provides an important link between Vedic astronomy and classical Hindu astronomy. In my book on Jain astronomy, important features of Jain astronomy have been discussed and compared with Vedic astronomy and classical Hindu astronomy. Based on the changing position of sun in the background of stars during solstices and equinoxes, the date of the astronomical observations described in Jain texts has been estimated. It is proposed that the zero point of Jain astronomy as well as Mālava era coincides with the yogatārā of Aświnī, Hamal, being at vernal equinox in 702 BCE.

As one of the inspirations of my work on Indian astronomy stems from my desire to understand the timing of the great astronomer Varāhamihira, this harmonization of Indian and western zodiacs firmly establishes Varāhmihira in the first century BCE, consistent with the Indian tradition that places him in the court of Emperor Vikramāditya. Once again, while Indian tradition fondly pays homage to the extraordinary valour of Emperor Vikramāditya in protecting India from the invaders by still counting time from 57 BCE called Vikrama era, yet regrettably many modern historians without evidence claim that there was no Vikramāditya in first century BCE. The search for Emperor Vikramāditya, in whose memory Vikrama era has been established, led me to reexamine the very foundations of Indian history. My books "India before Alexander: A New Chronology", "India after Alexander: The Age of

Vikramādityas", "India after Vikramāditya: The Melting Pot" and "An Alternative Timeline of Indian History: From Buddha and Mahavira to Bappa Rawal" detail an alternative timeline of Indian history derived from in-depth analysis of source materials. Most of the pre-Islamic chronology is based on counting backward and forward from two sheet anchors of Indian history - the identification of Sandrokottos of Greek accounts with Chandragupta Maurya and the identification of Devanampriya Priyadarshi of major rock edicts with Ashoka Maurya. With extensive background research, in my books I show that Sandrokottos of Greek accounts should be identified with Chandragupta I of Imperial Gupta dynasty and Devanampriya Priyadarshi of major rock edicts should be identified with Kumaragupta I, the great grandson of Chandragupta I.

In my work, I take extreme care in keeping my research transparent unlike some Indic researchers who give vague references and mislead readers by presenting their interpretations as evidence. In my books I fully explain the background needed to understand the subject matter, state of current scholarship, and why my thesis differs from others. You may or may not agree with my conclusions, but I hope that my books and articles will make you question the conventional history presented as facts with dubious evidence. This unscientific and dogmatic version of the history has been propagated by many Indic historians suffering from colonial mindset. It is also my sincere hope that my work will encourage others to use science as a critical tool to evaluate and understand Indian history.

www.ingramcontent.com/pod-product-compliance
Lightning Source LLC
Chambersburg PA
CBHW060744050426
42449CB00008B/1304
9781988207261